LAND

OF THE

RED SOIL

LAND

OF THE

RED SOIL

A
Popular
History
of
Prince
Edward
Island

DOUGLAS
BALDWIN

RAGWEED
THE ISLAND PUBLISHER

To my wife, Patty,
for her understanding,
support and love.

Second Printing, 2000

Main cover photograph: © John Sylvester
Inset cover photograph: © Barrett & MacKay Photography
Edited by: Jane Billinghurst
Printed and bound in Canada by: AGMV/Marquis

*With thanks to the Canada Council for the Arts
for its generous support.*

Published by:
Ragweed Press
P.O. Box 2023
Charlottetown, PEI
Canada C1A 7N7

Canadian Cataloguing in Publication Data
Baldwin, Douglas, 1944-
    Land of the red soil
    2nd ed.
    Includes index.
    ISBN 0-921556-72-1

1. Prince Edward Island — History. I. Title.

FC2611.B343 1998   971.7   C98-950010-1
F1048.B35 1998

Illustration acknowledgements: p. 120 — Robert Harris (1849-1919), *Soldiers*, 1918, graphite on paper, Collection of Confederation Centre Art Gallery and Museum, Gift of the Robert Harris Trust, 1965; p. 161 — "Women of Power," P.E.I. Government Photo — Brian L. Simpson; and p. 162 — "Debki Dancers," by Michael Rashed, from *A Stream Out of Lebanon* (Institute of Island Studies, 1988).

Illustration credit abbreviations: CCAGM — Confederation Centre Art Gallery and Museum; HC/CCAGM — Harris Collection, Confederation Centre Art Gallery and Museum; and PEIPARO — Prince Edward Island Public Archives and Records Office.

Contents

Preface

The study of history is a dynamic process; our knowledge of the past is constantly expanding as we find new sources and ask different questions of previously examined material. Sometimes, we witness history in the making: the decision to build a "fixed link" between Prince Edward Island and New Brunswick and the subsequent construction of the Confederation Bridge was such an occasion. For over a century, Islanders had debated the pros and cons of some permanent connection to the mainland; after a plebiscite, court challenges and prolonged negotiations, the construction of the longest bridge over ice-covered water in the world was completed in 1997, and history was made, with the world watching.

The first edition of *Land of the Red Soil* was published in 1990. This new and revised edition retains those aspects of the first edition that made it so popular, while benefiting from the discoveries and interpretations made by historians over the last decade. It includes several new chapters, updated statistics, and an expanded discussion of such topics as the reasons for the growth of Japanese tourists (in 1995, Japanese publishing house Kawade Shobo Shinsha published a Japanese edition of *Land of the Red Soil*); the role of women; the economy and the environment; education and public health; the life of Lucy Maud Montgomery; and, of course, the Confederation Bridge.

I hope you enjoy reading this new and revised *Land of the Red Soil* as much as I have enjoyed researching P.E.I. history.

Douglas Baldwin
History Department
Acadia University
March 1998

INTRODUCTION

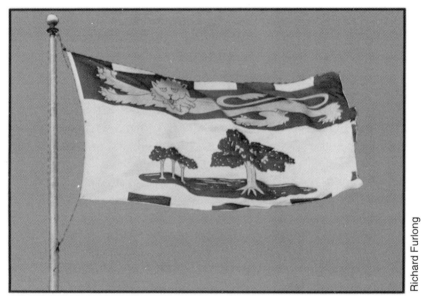

The Prince Edward Island flag

Welcome Home

"**W**elcome home!" Whether you are a native Islander or it is your first visit to Prince Edward Island, this is the invariable greeting. To all Islanders, whether or not they still live on the Island, this is home. Here they are surrounded by hundreds of uncles, nephews, nieces and other relatives.

To its inhabitants, Prince Edward Island is known simply as "The Island," as if it were the only one in the world. The Mi'kmaq called it *Minegoo*, which means "The Island," or more romantically, *Abegweit* — "cradled on the waves." Lucy Maud Montgomery, the famous author of the *Anne of Green Gables* children's stories, wrote in 1891, "He said he was from 'the island!' What island, queried a listener? 'What island?' repeated our honest countryman, in amazement. 'Why, Prince Edward Island, man! What other Island is there?' "

Those people unfortunate enough to have been born elsewhere are from "off-Island," or more commonly, "from away." A person's last name is often a clue that he or she is not Island-born. The telephone book lists page after page of Arsenaults, Gallants, Macs and Mcs, but contains only a smattering of family names that do not have Celtic, English or French roots. With 81 percent of its population of British origin and 14 percent of French descent, P.E.I. is the most homogeneous province in Canada. Islanders distinguish between families with the same last name by their geographical location. "Oh, you're one of the Souris MacDonalds," someone might say to identify a new friend.

Islanders are proud of their heritage, as the large number of local history books attest. Radio programs regale listeners with stories from the Island's past. The people cherish their history and are proud of their present. They do not wish to live anywhere else, nor,

Colourful Island Language

Many Islanders sprinkle their spoken language with a variety of fascinating and colourful words and phrases that give their conversation a flavour of its own.

back door trots:	diarrhea
bedlunch:	a light snack at bedtime
by times:	from time to time
catawampus:	out of order, mixed up
crowpiss:	very early in the morning
dead man's overcoat:	a coffin
great altogether:	fantastic
large day:	a day when one gets a lot done
lolly:	soft, floating snow
nosey weather:	a cold and windy day that makes the nose run
stormstayed:	stranded in one place because of heavy snow

generally, do they relish the idea of sampling other locales. Indeed, the Island is a good place to live. Violent crimes are uncommon and drug dealers are rare. There is no place to hide on a small island where everyone knows everyone else's business — or so it often seems. When Anne Shirley, of Montgomery's *Anne of Green Gables*, first arrived on the Island, she exclaimed, "I just love it already, and I'm so glad I'm going to live here. I've always heard that Prince Edward Island was the prettiest place in the world, and I used to imagine I was living here, but I never really expected I would. It's delightful when your imaginations come true, isn't it?"

Prince Edward Island is a crescent-shaped island of red sand, rolling green fields, neat rural settlements, pretty fishing villages and patchwork farms. It is possible to drive from one end to the other of the 224 kilometre-long (139 miles) island in half a day. The island is from 6 to 64 kilometres (4 to 40 miles) wide, and at the narrowest point, you can see from one shore to the other. The island is comparable in size to the State of Delaware or to Trinidad and Tobago. No one lives more than 16 kilometres (10 miles) from salt water.

The climate is temperate and few days are completely breezeless. The Island has a milder climate and more frost-free days than many other places in the Maritimes. Summers are warm but rarely humid, and visitors are comfortable in short-sleeved shirts during the day, with a cotton sweater or light jacket for evening. The waters surrounding the Island are excellent for swimming in July and August, when the daytime temperature sometimes rises into the 30s Centigrade. Winter begins early in December. Although the Island is often buffeted by snow storms and whipped by strong winds, the snow usually melts quickly.

Significant Island Facts

Population:	137,300 (0.5% of Canada)
Population Density:	23.6 persons per sq. km. (9.1 per sq. mi.; highest in Canada)
Capital:	Charlottetown (pop. 31,541)
First Languages:	English, 94%; French, 4%
Time Zone:	Atlantic (1 hour ahead of Toronto and New York)
Area:	5660 sq. km (2,185 sq. mi.)
Highest Point:	139.5 metres (460 feet)
Average Summer Temperature:	23°C (73.4°F)
Average January Temperature:	-3.5°C (25.7°F)
Average Annual Snowfall:	275 cm (123 in.)
Frost Free Days:	140 - 160 days
Annual Rainfall:	800 mm (31.5 in.)
Provincial Bird:	Blue Jay
Provincial Flower:	Lady Slipper Orchid
Provincial Tree:	Northern Red Oak
Provincial Song:	"The Island Hymn" by L. M. Montgomery
Provincial Motto:	Parva Sub Ingent: (The small under the protection of the great)
Entered Confederation:	1873
Members of Parliament:	Four
Senators:	Four

[P.E.I. Statistical Review, 1996 and Canada Year Book, 1997.]

From 8,600BC to the arrival of the first European settlers in the early seventeenth century, the Island was home to a series of nomadic peoples, who lived lightly on the land. The settlers greatly threatened the patterns of animal life on and around Prince Edward Island. Passenger pigeons, which were once so numerous that they blocked out the sun when they flew, are now extinct, as are the Great Auks. Once there were caribou, bear, moose and cougar, but now the largest wild animals are fox, beaver and raccoon. In the spring, tourists take helicopters to the ice floes around the Island to see baby white seals. Dolphins, sperm whales and minke whales can also be seen in Island waters. There are no poisonous snakes, and only a few species of reptiles and amphibians make their home on the Island. More than three hundred species of birds live on or pass through the Island including blue jays, owls and Canada Geese. Blue herons feed in shallow waters, and hawks cruise the shoreline dunes.

Since the beginning of European settlement on Prince Edward Island, the Island has often been viewed as one huge farm. Indeed, it has been called the "million acre farm." About 60 percent of the province is suitable for cultivation. The famous red topsoil is not very deep, but it is generally excellent for growing potatoes. In addition to planting table potatoes, Islanders grow potatoes for French fries and potato chips, and export seed potatoes around the world. P.E.I.'s major export market for potatoes is the United States, followed by Venezuela, France, Trinidad, Japan and Italy.

The region's most prominent natural resource is the ocean, which has given the area its name (maritime) and its historic and geographic identity. Fishing vessels from as far away as Japan and Poland sail to the Maritimes for the offshore fishery. Huge factory freezer trawlers process as well as catch fish, while thousands of smaller inshore vessels harvest the ocean nearer land. Live lobsters, fresh fish and shellfish are exported to the United States; and canned, dried, frozen, smoked and pickled fish are sold in Europe, the Caribbean and the Far East.

In recent years the fishery has been particularly hard hit. Over-fishing, by both foreign and domestic ships, and low market prices have left Maritime fishers with drastically reduced incomes. Beginning in the early twentieth century, limits were placed on who could fish, where they could fish and when fishing was allowed. Poaching,

The Island Economy

GDP: $2.648 billion

GDP Per Capita: $19,328

Agriculture: potatoes, dairy products, cattle, hogs, strawberries, blueberries. Farm cash receipts: $294.4 million. Potatoes contribute over 50 percent of total receipts. Only 6 percent of Islanders now live on farms. Island farmland is the most expensive in Canada. Major problems: soil erosion and pesticides.

Fisheries: lobster, crab, herring cod, hake, mussels, clams, oysters, salmon, trout, Irish Moss. Total fish landings: $104.7 million, of which $65.8 million was lobster. Major problems: overfishing, pollution.

Tourism: in 1997, 1.24 million tourists spent over $262 million. Tourism employs about 18 percent of the provincial workforce and is the second-largest industry. The largest number of tourists come from Atlantic Canada (35%), Quebec (7%), New England States (7%) and a surprising number come from Japan (only 1% in 1997 due to economic difficulties in Asia-Pacific). Major problems: land use changes, environmental damages.

Forestry: the original forests were high-quality hardwoods — sugar maple, yellow birch and beech. Today's forest is split between softwood (conifers, white spruce) and hardwoods (poplar, red maple and white birch). Recent demand for construction-grade lumber and pulpwood has brought renewed interest in silviculture. Total forest production: $25.1 million. Major problems: reforestation, clearcutting and poor quality forests.

Manufacturing: transportation equipment, fabricated metal products, chemicals, food, fish and wood products. Total value of shipment of manufactured goods: $641.6 million. Major problems: monopoly concentration.

[P.E.I. Statistical Review, 1996 and Economic Impact: Tourism, 1997.]

foreign fishers operating beyond Canadian control, and the growing demand for fish and shellfish gradually reduced the stock of fish. To allow time for the fish to replenish themselves, in 1992 the federal government slashed the number of fish that could be harvested and offered income supplements to the fishers. Anticipating these problems, Maritime governments are attempting to develop markets for such underutilized species as hake, herring and mackerel. In addition, scientific culturing of mussels, oysters, salmon, soft-shell clams and trout have made aquaculture a booming business.

Tourism flourished in the 1950s and 1960s as people began to have more leisure time and the money to travel. The red soil, green fields and blue ocean of the Island offer a panorama of beautiful scenic contrasts. Vacationers are attracted by the warm, sandy beaches. The national park on the north shore is second in popularity only to Banff National Park in Alberta. Its 40 kilometres (25 miles) of scenic coastline include spectacular sand dunes, sandstone cliffs, freshwater ponds, salt marshes and woodlands. This is the area of the Island immortalized in Lucy Maud Montgomery's book, *Anne of Green Gables.*

Tourists find P.E.I. a friendly place, and come to relax and forget the troubles of big-city living. During the summer of 1997, more than one million visitors came to the Island. This was more than seven times the Island's total population. To serve the growing number of tourists, the Island provides more than six thousand hotels and bed-and-breakfasts, over fifty public and private campgrounds, fifteen golf courses and seventeen provincial and federal parks.

Prince Edward Island politics reflect the narrow confines of the Island. The provincial legislature is smaller than either the Montreal or Toronto city councils. Local political meetings are well attended, and the province traditionally has one of the highest voter turnouts in the country. Historically, the Liberals and Conservatives have been the elected representatives of Islanders, with governments changing back and forth after a term or two. Only in 1996 was the first New Democrat elected to the P.E.I. legislature. Political issues are often dominated by discussions over patronage, and most people feel a personal connection to their party of choice. Indeed, the promise of patronage jobs is a powerful incentive at election time.

ONE

The First Islanders

A Mi'kmaq Legend

A long time ago, the Great Spirit, who lived in the Happy Hunting Grounds, created the universe and all life. The Wise One enjoyed his creation in the twinkling lights of thousands of stars, the sun and the many galaxies in the universe.

After creating the universe, the Great Spirit sat down to rest. Then he created Glooscap and gave him special spiritual and physical powers. He called Glooscap to share the sacred pipe and said, "Glooscap, I am going to create people in my own image. I will call them Micmac."

The Great Spirit was pleased with this creation. He took out his sacred pipe and again called Glooscap. As the Great Spirit was smoking he noticed a large amount of dark red clay left over. "Glooscap, look at this large piece of clay, the same colour as my Micmac people. I will shape this clay into a crescent form and it will be the most beautiful of all places on Mother Earth. It will become the home of my Micmac people."

The Great Spirit fashioned an enchanting island and called it Minegoo. He dressed her dark red skin with green grass and lush forests of many different kinds of trees, and sprinkled her with many brightly coloured flowers. Her forest floors were like deep soft carpets that would cushion the moccasined feet of the Micmac people.

Minegoo was so beautiful that it made the Great Spirit extremely happy — so happy that he thought about placing Minegoo among the stars. After considering this for a short time, the Wise One decided that Minegoo should be placed in the middle of the singing waters, now known as the Gulf of St. Lawrence.

John Joe Sark
Micmac Legends of Prince Edward Island,
Ragweed Press, 1988, p. 6

This Mi'kmaq creation story parallels the Christian allegory in Genesis. Both tales depict the almighty ruler as a male and place humans on the land at the time of its creation. Scientists from several different disciplines, however, have established that Prince Edward Island was slowly fashioned over centuries, and only comparatively recently has it been inhabited by humans. In fact, if the history of the universe was compressed into a one-year period, humans would appear only on the very last day.

Three hundred million years ago, Prince Edward Island and the Northumberland Strait did not exist. Rivers flowing from mountain ranges in New Brunswick, Nova Scotia and Quebec deposited small particles of rock, silt and clay on the lowland region leading to the present-day Gulf of St. Lawrence. Over millions of years, layers of these particles, called sediments, created a low-lying plain. When the waters of the gulf rose, flooding the plain, an island appeared. The weight of the upper layers of sediment compressed the lower layers of sediment into rock. Small amounts of iron in the upper sediments rusted on contact with water and air and left a red stain on the surrounding particles. This explains the Island's red soil.

For millions of years the Island enjoyed a mild climate. Then, one or two million years ago, temperatures dropped. The snow no longer melted in the summer, and as it accumulated over the years, its immense weight compressed the lower layers of snow into ice. In some areas in western Prince Edward Island, the ice was 1,000 metres (3,280 feet) deep. These glaciers were so heavy that they depressed the land below sea level.

The glaciers of the last ice age began melting about eighteen thousand years ago. As the ice melted, the sea level rose higher than it is today. Parts of Prince Edward Island were flooded, and the land was divided into three separate islands. Once the weight of the glaciers was gone, the land slowly rebounded. Then, between eleven thousand and six thousand years ago, as the sea level fell to almost 40 metres (130 feet) below its present height, the Northumberland Strait disappeared and the Island became part of the mainland. Gradually, the water began to rise, and about three thousand years ago the Island was again separated from the mainland.

As the glaciers melted, they left behind a covering of broken rock, gravel, sand, silt and clay. Large boulders, originally from the mainland, were carried by the glaciers and dropped on the west end of the Island near Poplar Grove and Kildare River. The first plants to grow after the ground thawed were lichens and mosses. They eventually died, decayed, became humus and helped support additional plant life. The dying plants mixed with the clay, sand and silt to form the Island's topsoil. Partly because the glacial deposits were acidic, the Island soil also became acidic and to this day is deficient in natural fertility.

The only records of the Island's prehistoric plants and animals exist in the small fossils that are occasionally found along the beaches. Recent discoveries in Nova Scotia suggest that large mastodons inhabited this area of the world between ten thousand and seventy thousand years ago. Perhaps the most fascinating discovery was made near French River in 1845. In that year, in the process of digging a well, several men uncovered the fossil of a *Bathygnathus borealis* that had been alive about 280 million years ago. This reptile in the Pelycosaur family was about 2 metres (6 feet) long and sported a large fin or "sail" on its back.

Early Peoples

What we know about early Island peoples has been pieced together from Native legends; accounts written by European missionaries, explorers and fur traders; and archaeological explorations. Archaeologists examine weapon points, tools and pottery fragments to interpret the past. Geologists use glacier spoors to establish when and where the glaciers existed. Physicists measure the amount of carbon 14 in once-living matter to determine its age. Botanists analyze pollen traces to date campsites and describe ancient vegetation cycles, and climatologists plot the weather through the centuries.

One problem in discussing early Mi'kmaq life is accurately interpreting the written evidence left by explorers, fur traders and missionaries, who judged the Mi'kmaq according to their own cultural standards. Fur traders in search of beaver pelts, for example, believed that Mi'kmaq who did not actively pursue these animals were lazy. Priests, unfamiliar with the beliefs of the Aboriginal people, decided that the Mi'kmaq had no religion. In need of money from France, the Jesuits misrepresented the Mi'kmaq, describing them as "savage" in order to emphasize the difficulty of their task. Current concerns also influence how people interpret the past. Mi'kmaq and government researchers concerned with Aboriginal land claims, for example, often turn to the past for supporting arguments.

Human occupation of the Maritimes probably began about 10,600 years ago (8,600 B.C.) with people who most likely migrated from the New England region after the glaciers had receded. Archaeologists refer to these peoples as the Paleo-Indians. At this time, the Island was still joined to the mainland, the climate was much colder than it is today, and the vegetation was sparser. The Paleo-Indians employed a unique style of spear point, and hunted caribou, arctic foxes and hares. Those groups that lived near the coastline took advantage of the variety of fish and birds that frequented the area. Spears used to kill caribou could also kill seals and walrus. Unfortunately, we do not know what language these people spoke, what tools they employed or much about their daily lives. Equally frustrating is the fact that we do not know what happened to them.

From about 9,000 to 3,500 years ago, peoples with a slightly different way of life inhabited the Maritimes. This period, called the Maritime Archaic Age, was more sea oriented, and the Aboriginal peoples had a well-developed culture. They fashioned delicately carved bone and stone figures of birds and whales, and made bone whistles and hair combs. As the population expanded, the Maritime Archaic people built homes as large as 100 metres (328 feet) in length, which they divided into separate family units. These people might have been descendants of the Paleo-Indians or perhaps a different group who had migrated northward into the forests of coniferous and hardwood trees that took root as the climate warmed. Approximately 10,000 years ago, for example, spruce and birch predominated in the Maritime region; 3,000 years later, the forests consisted of pine, oak and birch; and by the time the Norsemen arrived around 1,000 A.D., the land was covered by birch, hemlock, pine, fir, maple and spruce.

Unfortunately, submerged coastlines have obliterated the remains of many Aboriginal campsites. The Island sandstone, being a soft rock, is easily eroded by ice, wave and wind action. This erosion, combined with a gradually rising sea level, means that every year the coastline recedes from several centimetres (1 inch) to a few metres (several feet), depending upon location. During the last century, as the sea level continued to rise, the Maritime provinces submerged by almost 30 centimetres (13.5 inches), giving rise to predictions of future calamities. Since the original inhabitants preferred to be near the water because of its store of wildlife, many of their campsites are now probably underwater. Just as their predecessors had done, the Maritime Archaic peoples apparently disappeared without a trace.

The Mi'kmaq

When the first Europeans arrived in the Maritimes there were about eighteen thousand Aboriginal people in the area. The Mi'kmaq occupied Nova Scotia, Prince Edward Island and eastern New Brunswick. As far as we can tell, the Mi'kmaq did not develop permanent settlements on the Island, but assembled here in the summer to fish; to hunt for waterfowl, seals and small whales; and to gather shellfish and periwinkles. Many of the existing remnants of Mi'kmaq life were discovered in shell middens. These heaps of sea shells discarded by the Mi'kmaq changed the chemical composition of the soil and preserved bones and other organic matter that the Island's acidic soil would otherwise have destroyed. Archaeologists have discovered Mi'kmaq sites in the Malpeque and Rustico Bay areas, Savage Harbour, and the North and South Lakes region. The area between Souris and East Point seems to have held a special attraction for the Mi'kmaq.

Life in the wigwam

Although the Mi'kmaq used local stones found on the beaches, the best materials for fashioning tools, knives and arrowheads existed on the mainland; the Mi'kmaq must have travelled there frequently in their wooden canoes. These vessels, fashioned out of birch and cedar, measured up to 8 metres (27 feet) in length. Spruce gum, first chewed by women and girls to make it pliable and then boiled with fat, was used to waterproof the canoes. The Mi'kmaq were skilled woodworkers. They made ingeniously constructed wooden cradleboards that rested on the mother's back and were supported by a strap across her forehead, which left her arms free for work and protected the child from tree branches. Inside the wigwam, the cradleboard was propped up so the infant could see its surroundings. With similar ingenuity, the Mi'kmaq also crafted spears, bows and arrows, traps, axes, snowshoes, fish weirs and toboggans.

Mi'kmaq wigwams varied in size and shape depending upon individual preference and family size. A young couple with one or two small children might live in a small circular wigwam, whereas a larger family would construct a large oval or triangular wigwam. In the summer, woven reed or grass mats covered these wood-framed structures. During dry weather, the reeds shrank and allowed more air to flow through the mats, thus keeping the interior cool and smoke-free. When it rained, the reeds swelled and the wigwam became watertight. Animal hides kept the homes warm and cozy in the winter.

Since the wigwams had no separate rooms, the Mi'kmaq devised rules to ensure privacy. Each family member was assigned a special place in the wigwam. The parents slept at the back. The youngest children were next to their parents — girls on one side, boys on the other. The older children spent the night near the entrance, which would have been the draftiest and busiest section in the dwelling. When a person sat next to the fireplace, it meant that he or she wanted to talk and be sociable. Sitting against the wall, however, indicated a desire to be left alone.

The Mi'kmaq enjoyed singing and dancing, and organized frequent feasts. Adults played a game with a ball stuffed with animal hair and grass. Teammates tossed the ball back and forth, seeking to touch it against their opponent's post at the opposite end of the playing field. A gambling game called *waltes* was popular with all ages and both sexes. It involved tossing six two-sided discs, not unlike dice, into a shallow bowl. Points were scored depending upon whether the light or dark side faced upwards. The discs were made of stone, bone or pottery, and were often handsomely decorated. Music and dancing were popular at feasts. Instruments included bone flutes, rolled birchbark and rattles made of fish skins and filled with gravel. Storytelling played an important role as well. In addition to providing amusement, the tales passed on the tribe's history and cultural beliefs to future generations.

Several times each summer, the people of neighbouring villages met for special occasions. Here, young men and women courted, and the adults arranged hunting boundaries and planned raids on enemy villages. Although each village had civil and religious leaders, all Mi'kmaq were free to decide for themselves whether to accede to their leaders' decisions. Mi'kmaq were never forced to do anything against their will; customs and peer pressure ensured an orderly society.

The most important activity, of course, was earning a living, which meant hunting, trapping, fishing, and gathering roots and berries. To catch beavers in the winter, hunters used a stone chisel to cut holes in the ice covering the beaver ponds and stood quietly nearby, waiting to harpoon or spear the beavers as they emerged from the holes. Another technique involved cutting a hole in a beaver lodge and clubbing the hibernating rodents before they could escape. Moose were hunted on snowshoes. The larger the animal a Mi'kmaq hunter caught, the greater his reputation. During the summer, the Mi'kmaq relied on aquatic life for sustenance.

The women, in addition to mending and sewing, also did the cooking. They placed red-hot stones from the fire into large wooden cooking kettles. When the water boiled, the women added meat, fish or shellfish. More heated rocks were added when necessary. Meat was roasted on a spit. They used stone hammers to crush seal and moose bones. The pulp was boiled, and as the fat rose to the surface it was skimmed off into a bark container to harden. This solid fat provided nutritious food on long journeys. Hot fat was considered a delicious beverage. Animal fat and birds' eggs made excellent paints, with which the Mi'kmaq decorated their bodies and painted their clothes, wigwams, tools, bowls and ornaments.

The Mi'kmaq shared with other Aboriginal peoples a special relationship with nature. The woods and fields were an extension of themselves. The Mi'kmaq were so close to the animals they hunted that they could imitate their sounds, and hunters were often named after the animals they had slain. In the Mi'kmaq world, every object had a spirit. Humans were not considered superior in nature; they were equal partners with animals and plants, the sun, the wind, and the rain. The hunter would thus apologize to an animal for taking its life. The dead animal's carcass was treated with respect and handled according to prescribed rituals, lest its spirit warn its fellows to leave the area. According to legend, Glooscap told the Mi'kmaq:

> *If you have to kill a deer so that you can live, you should tell the deer that his beauty will live on to glorify the Great Spirit in the clothing that will be made out of its skin. The skin must be carefully treated and decorated so that it is worthy of the Great Spirit. All parts of the deer should be shared among the Mi'kmaq people and anything not used should be hung on a tree so that it will not be desecrated. Thanks must then be given to the Great Spirit for the use of the deer.*

By the end of the 1400s, giant boats carrying strangely garbed people from Europe began to visit the Gulf of St. Lawrence. At first, these people with pale skins and hairy bodies came ashore only to acquire drinking water and firewood. They sometimes offered gifts of brightly coloured cloth or left metal goods that were stronger than the copper the Mi'kmaq obtained from the mainland. Soon, the Mi'kmaq began to exchange gifts with these strangers, who seemed to be particularly enamoured of the Mi'kmaq's beaver-skin clothing. The coming of these visitors would change the ancient pattern of Mi'kmaq life.

TWO

Pioneer Acadian women

Media Services, Halifax

Île St. Jean

In the fifteenth century, Spain, Portugal, France and England were eager to establish trade routes to the new-found riches of Asia. Spanish navigator Christopher Columbus believed that it was possible to sail around the world to Asia and that it would take about a week. In 1492 he set sail across the Atlantic and, after a seventy-day journey, came unexpectedly across the Americas.

The wealth discovered by Columbus and the explorers who followed him to the New World made Spain the envy of other nations. England, Portugal and France decided to hire their own explorers to find kingdoms as rich as those the Spaniards had discovered in Central and South America. In 1534, King Francis I of France instructed Jacques Cartier to "discover certain isles where it is said there must be great quantities of gold and other riches" and to seek a trade route to Asia. Cartier thus became the first European to visit Prince Edward Island and leave a written record of his trip.

It took Cartier only twenty days to cross the Atlantic. Off the coast of Newfoundland, the explorer sighted a group of Great Auks. "Some of these birds," Cartier wrote, "are as large as geese, being black and white with a beak like a crow. They are always in the water, being unable to fly, since they have tiny wings about half the size of your hand ... These birds are marvelously fat ... and in less than half an hour our longboats were loaded with them. Each of our ships salted four or five casks, not to mention those we ate fresh." Easy to catch, tasty to eat and good for fishing bait, the last Great Auk was killed in 1844.

After exploring the west coast of Newfoundland, Cartier sailed to the Magdalen Islands, where he encountered "many great beasts, like large oxen, which have two tusks in their jaws like elephants' tusks, and swim about in the water." Leaving these sea lions, Cartier sighted Prince Edward Island on June 29, 1534. He spent the next two days exploring the north coast, which he believed was part of the mainland. At Malpeque, Cartier wrote, "We went ashore in our longboats at several places, and among others at a fine river of little depth, where we caught sight of some Indians in their canoes who were crossing the river. On that account we named this river Canoe River."

Cartier left a vivid description of the landscape. "We landed that day," he continued, "in four places to see the trees which were wonderfully beautiful and very fragrant. We discovered that there were cedars, yew-trees, pines, white elms, ash trees, willows and others, many of them unknown to us and all trees without fruit. The soil where there are no trees is also very rich and is covered with peas, white and red gooseberry bushes, strawberries, raspberries and wild oats like rye ... It is the best tempered region one can possibly see and the heat is considerable."

Cartier turned northward into the Miramichi River and sailed to the Gaspé Peninsula. Here he erected a large cross, claimed the land for King Francis I of France, and returned to France with two

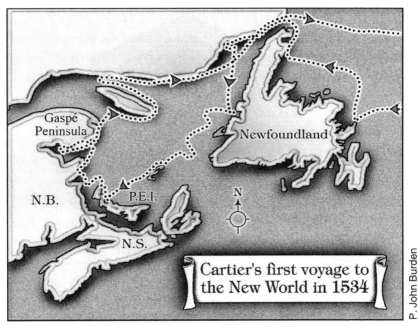

Cartier's first voyage to the New World

Mi'kmaq captives. Except for European fishing boats that may have stopped to trade with the Mi'kmaq or to collect drinking water, Europeans did not revisit Prince Edward Island for another 70 years.

Although Cartier and other explorers did not find silks, spices or precious minerals in Canada, the New World soon became very important to Europe. Fishers from England, France, Spain, Portugal and Holland continued to come each spring to catch cod off the Grand Banks of Newfoundland, in the Gulf of St. Lawrence and in the Bay of Fundy. It is said that the cod were so plentiful that they sometimes slowed the progress of the fishing boats.

Fish was a major part of the diet of most Europeans. Roman Catholics were forbidden to eat meat on Fridays in memory of Christ's death on Good Friday. There were also about one hundred and fifty other days each year designated meatless by the Roman Catholic church. Since fish was not considered meat, it was in great demand. Fish was also important to the economy of Great Britain, and the British government had declared certain days fish days to encourage its consumption. The importance of fish helps to explain why England and France fought so frequently for control of the Maritimes in the seventeenth and eighteenth centuries.

While the European fishers were on shore salting the cod they had caught, they took the opportunity to trade with the Mi'kmaq. The Mi'kmaq exchanged beaver, caribou, otter and other furs for guns, metal tools, axes, kettles and bright clothing. Beaver hats were fashionable in Europe at the time, and everyone wanted one. As styles kept changing, beaver skins were in constant demand. Although the Europeans had initially come to North America in search of a route to Asia, they now came for fish and furs. Soon settlers would join the fishers and fur traders.

Acadia

To safeguard its supply of furs and cod, France decided to establish a colony in North America. In 1604, the King of France, Henry IV, granted Sieur de Monts present-day Nova Scotia, New Brunswick, Prince Edward Island, and parts of

Quebec and the eastern United States. The grant included the right to fish and trade with the Natives. In return, de Monts promised to bring settlers to the area.

The first group of French colonists, led by Samuel de Champlain, Jean de Poutrincourt and Pierre du Gua de Monts, sailed into the Bay of Fundy in 1604 and established the colony of Port Royal (now Annapolis Royal, Nova Scotia). With the help of the Mi'kmaq, Port Royal grew and prospered. Additional settlements were built along the shores and around the head of the Bay of Fundy. By the beginning of the eighteenth century, the inhabitants had developed a distinctive identity. The settlers called their new home L'Acadie and before long became known as Acadians.

Life was not always peaceful for the Acadians. For most of the 1600s, England and France were at war in Europe, and these conflicts frequently spread to North America. France argued that Acadia was French territory because Jacques Cartier had been the first European to land there. England claimed that John Cabot was the first European to discover Acadia and that the land was therefore British territory. England and France were willing to spill blood for Acadia because of its proximity to the rich fishing grounds of the Grand Banks and its strategic location between the newly settled colonies of New France and New England. In its first 100 years of existence, Acadia changed hands nine times and was attacked by British troops ten additional times. The Acadians were caught in the middle, not wanting to fight for either the French or the British. They wished to be left alone to tend their fields.

The year 1713 was a turning point in the history of Acadia. The war with Great Britain had gone poorly for France. In the Treaty of Utrecht, which followed the defeat of France, Great Britain kept present-day Nova Scotia, New Brunswick and Newfoundland. France retained New France (Quebec), Île Royale (Cape Breton), Île St. Jean (Prince Edward Island) and the right to land its ships on the north coast of Newfoundland.

To protect its territories, France decided to build a stone fortress, Louisbourg, on an ice-free harbour to control entry to the St. Lawrence River and to monitor the fishery off the Grand Banks. Unfortunately, the land surrounding Louisbourg was infertile, and the area was wind-swept and fog-bound for much of the year.

Construction began in 1720 and continued for twenty-five years. According to rumour, King Louis XV once joked that with all the money he had spent, he expected to see the fortress on the horizon.

When Great Britain gained control of Acadia in 1713, the Acadians were told to swear allegiance to the British Crown or leave. For its part, France tried to persuade the Acadians living in Nova Scotia to move to Île Royale. The more people living there, the stronger it would be against a British attack. However, most Acadians decided to remain where they were. Acadia was their homeland, and they had put too much work into their land to leave. Britain had captured Acadia several times before and had returned it to France, and the Acadians hoped that this would happen once again. In 1719, King Louis XV decided to open Île St. Jean for settlement. If the Acadians would not leave their farms for Île Royale, perhaps they would come to the Island, where the soil was more fertile. Farmers on Île St. Jean could provide food for the troops at Louisbourg. A new era was dawning for Prince Edward Island.

A 1734 design for the fort at Port LaJoye
(National Archives of Canada)

Île St. Jean

Following Cartier's voyage in 1534, Europeans ignored Île St. Jean until King Louis XIV of France granted it to Sieur de Monts in 1604. De Monts, however, did not bring the promised settlers to the Island. In 1653, King Louis XIV of France granted control of the Island to Nicolas Denys in return for Denys' promise to settle eighty Roman Catholic families there. Ten years later, Denys had not brought any colonists to the Island and the king awarded it to Sieur François Doublet. When Doublet also failed to live up to his promises, King Louis XV gave Île St. Jean to Gabriel Gauthier, and, in 1719, to Comte (Count) de Saint Pierre.

Finally, in April 1720, approximately 250 colonists set out from France to the Island with supplies of grain, livestock, tools and clothing. Four months later, the ships sailed into Port LaJoye (across the Hillsborough Harbour from present-day Charlottetown). In the next few years, the colonists established several settlements along the coast, the largest of which were at St. Peter's Harbour, Tracadie, Savage Harbour, Malpeque and Trois Rivières (present-day Brudenell Point). Port LaJoye became the capital of the Island, and a garrison of thirty ill-equipped men guarded the entrance to the harbour. The main purpose of the settlement, as far as France was concerned, was to grow food for the fort at Louisbourg. The mainland Acadians, however, did not find the Island as fertile as their own land and were no more eager to move there than they had been to move to Île Royale. By 1730, there were only 325 settlers on the Island, most of them recent immigrants from France.

Jean Pierre Roma

Jean Pierre Roma was one of the few people at this time who thought that Île St. Jean had a bright future. He was born in France in the seventeenth century, but no one knows exactly where or when. Where and when he died is also unknown. We do know that Roma founded a colony at Trois Rivières in 1732 and became one of the most important men on Île St. Jean. Roma was honest and hard working; however, he was also stubborn, quick to anger and hated criticism. He was full of dreams for the Island's future, but his plans for Trois Rivières were destroyed by bad luck and his inability to deal with people.

Roma was one of the directors of the Company of the East, formed by a group of French businesspeople to colonize Île St. Jean. In 1731, King Louis XV gave the Company the land drained by the Cardigan, Brudenell and Montague Rivers in return for the

Company's agreement to establish a colony on the Island. Roma arrived on the Island in 1732 with about three hundred people. He chose to settle the land at Trois Rivières.

In the following two years, Roma personally looked after the colony's growth. To improve the harbour, the men levelled the shoreline and built a pier, which meant moving more than 195 metric tonnes of rock by hand. The men cleared the nearby fields of timber, removed more than six thousand stumps, levelled the land, and built nine houses, two of which were twenty-four metres (78 feet) long. The settlers planted vegetable gardens around every building, and surrounded the gardens with brush-wood fences to keep animals out. They planted cabbages, turnips, wheat and peas, and harvested the sea.

The Tracadie Families of 1752

In one small area, Tracadie Harbour, eight families settled on the west side of the harbour, and cleared the land to the east for their crops of wheat, barley and peas. Their livestock grazed on the grassy meadows to the south.

The families made their living by farming the land and fishing for cod. Often, three generations lived together in one household, and all family members assisted in the numerous tasks of these labour-intensive activities.

The census of 1752 was carried out on the Island by Sieur de la Roque. He was asked to record the names, ages and professions of all settlers and their children, and the amount of cleared land and number of livestock. Further instructions asked him to inspect the coast for places where troops could be most easily landed, to give the size and condition of harbours and to conduct "a general survey of everything."

Family Name:	Number of Children
Galland (Jacques):	7
Boudrot (Charles):	4
Bourg (Charles):	12
Boudrot (Pierre):	2
Bourg (Michel):	7
Boudrot (François):	6
Boudrot (Claude):	6
Belliveaux (Louis):	6

Roma's colonists traded their goods with the other settlements on the Island. The route by sea, however, was long, and the frequent storms were dangerous for the small fishing vessels. If the colony was to survive, roads had to be built. Roma set his men to work cutting two-metre-wide (6.5 feet) bush paths through the wilderness to connect Trois Rivières with Cardigan, Souris, Sturgeon River, St. Peter's Harbour and the capital at Port LaJoye. Writing about the path from Trois Rivières to Port LaJoye, Roma said, "Most of the trees lying on the ground across the road have been left where they lie, since it is easy enough to step over them."

Despite Roma's two years of hard work, the other directors of the Company of the East were not pleased with the colony's progress. They wanted profits, but in the first year Trois Rivières had cost twice as much money to operate as it earned. Unwilling to weather a few lean years, the directors refused to pay for more provisions, and they blamed Roma for the colony's lack of success. For example, they claimed that Roma had used fishers to build roads rather than allowing them to fish. They felt he had spent too much money on the colony, when he should have been looking for ways of making a profit. Roma also argued with the settlers and destroyed their enthusiasm — or so the directors stated. We do know that Roma refused to attend weddings and baptisms. These events were the centre of the colony's social life, and his reluctance to attend upset many of the settlers. When the Company of the East decided to rid itself of this "burden," Roma bought the Company's land on Île St. Jean in 1737.

Roma's problems with the Catholic priests at the settlement are another example of his inability to get along with people. The Company had sent two priests to Trois Rivières with the first settlers. Roma disliked them both. He especially distrusted Abbé de Bierne, who was just as stubborn as Roma. De Bierne insisted that the people should not be forced to work on Sundays and other holy days. Roma stated that there was too much work to be done to allow for rest on Sundays, and argued that he had the King's authority to make laws for his colony. De Bierne claimed to have divine authority and informed the settlers that they were to follow his instructions in matters of religion. After a bitter struggle, Roma forced the Abbé to leave. Shortly afterwards, Roma dismissed the remaining priest.

Bad luck also afflicted the settlement. In 1736, fire destroyed most of the crops. Two years later, a plague of field mice ate the entire crop. Not long after this, Roma's cargo vessel was ship-wrecked. These disasters forced Roma to borrow money to keep the colony afloat. Finally, in 1745, just when the future was beginning to look promising, British troops attacked Trois Rivières.

The Mice Invasion

The Acadian settlers on P.E.I. often suffered plagues of grasshoppers, mosquitoes and mice. Mice were a constant problem. They lived in the forests and stored seeds, nuts and grasses for the winter. Every six weeks, the females produced litters of between ten and twelve young. When the snow was deep for several winters in a row, the mice population multiplied rapidly. In spring, the starving mice streamed out of the forest in long narrow columns.

They ate everything in their way. The mice destroyed crops and ate the food set aside for livestock. They swarmed over the grassy fields, and when the mice came to a river, those in the front were pushed on by those behind, and the river became choked with dead bodies. So numerous were these tiny invaders that nearby ships were slowed by the huge masses of drowned mice.

Plagues of mice destroyed crops in 1724, 1728, 1738 and 1749. Each time this happened the settlers had to rely on Louisbourg for food and seeds. The town of Souris, which means "mouse" in French, was named in memory of these plagues.

The British attack was part of the continuing struggle between France and Great Britain. As had happened so often before, the fighting began in Europe and spread around the world. Great Britain desired complete control over both the Atlantic fisheries and the fur trade along the St. Lawrence River. The British colonists living in New England wished also to stop the French settlers and their Mi'kmaq allies from raiding and looting their villages. To achieve these goals, Louisbourg, France's fortress on Île Royale, had to be captured.

In 1745, with the help of the American colonies, Great Britain used its superior naval power to capture Louisbourg. Some of its ships then sailed from New England to Île St. Jean and destroyed the French settlements at Trois Rivières and Port LaJoye. Roma's colony did not resist. Having only one cannon for defence, Roma and his settlers fled into the woods. They watched helplessly from the forest as the British set their homes on fire and loaded the colony's livestock, tools and grain aboard ship, and set sail.

At Port LaJoye, the small garrison was understaffed and poorly equipped, and, as at Trois Rivières, the settlers retreated into the interior. As the British soldiers advanced into the woods, they were ambushed by a band of Mi'kmaq who had joined the French. The British invaders were driven back to their boats and later returned to Louisbourg. They left behind burned houses and crops — the ruins of the Island's capital.

Back in Trois Rivières, Roma's dreams were shattered. Faced with starvation, Roma sailed to New France. He remained there for three years before going to the West Indies. Roma wanted to return to Île St. Jean to start again; however, he had no money and the French officials would not help him. Jean Pierre Roma never returned. His work would be continued by others.

Unfulfilled Promise

The war lasted from 1745 to 1748. Neither side was completely victorious. Great Britain captured Île Royale in North America, but lost territory in other parts of the world. At the peace talks in 1748, Great Britain traded Louisbourg back to France for the Indian state of Madras. In North America, the situation reverted to what it had been in 1713.

For the first time, France began to take a serious interest in Île St. Jean and its plans to encourage the Acadians on the mainland, which was still a British possession, to move to the Island. The Acadians were still reluctant to leave their farms; however, when Great Britain demanded that the Acadians promise to fight in all future North American wars against France, many decided to move to Île St. Jean. New settlements began at present-day Pownal, Orwell, Pinette, Crapaud, Tryon, Covehead and Malpeque. Although Île St. Jean was still seen mainly as a provisioning post for Louisbourg, it was finally showing signs of real progress.

Between 1748 and 1751 the population of Île St. Jean tripled to more than two thousand people. To ensure that the garrison at Louisbourg was well fed, King Louis XV ordered the Islanders to refrain from fishing because, he declared, it detracted from farming. The Island, however, had few natural meadows, and the Acadians were forced into the backbreaking work of clearing the forest for farmland. The typical farm had a few oxen, cows, pigs, sheep and chickens. Wheat, peas and oats were the most common crops. Île St. Jean, however, never fulfilled its role as a supplier of provisions for Louisbourg. Forest fires, wheat rust, and plagues of mice and grasshoppers on the Island meant that Louisbourg often had to supply the settlers with food, lest they starve. The Acadians' dietary staples consisted of pea soup; bread or porridge; salted beef, pork, mutton and fowl; maple syrup; herbs and garden vegetables; fish and game. Men and women smoked tobacco, and the women chewed spruce gum, which aided digestion and cleansed the teeth.

THREE

A missionary's visit

The Mi'kmaq and the Acadians

The Mi'kmaq

The first Europeans to contact the Mi'kmaq were fishers who had come to catch cod. In the seventeenth century, France established trading posts in present-day Nova Scotia and New Brunswick. Because there were no trading posts on Île St. Jean, the Island Mi'kmaq canoed to the mainland posts and also traded with French ships that anchored offshore in the summer. Firing their guns into the air, the French traders greeted the Mi'kmaq with great ceremony.

The Europeans believed that they were superior to the Mi'kmaq. The Mi'kmaq wore few clothes and their technology seemed inferior to that of the Europeans, who had guns and sophisticated tools. Unable to understand the Mi'kmaq language, Europeans judged the people by their material possessions and found them wanting. French priests, unfamiliar with Mi'kmaq beliefs, decided that they were heathens who had to be converted and "civilized." Not surprisingly, the Mi'kmaq considered themselves superior to the Europeans, who were unable to canoe or snowshoe very far before becoming exhausted and who performed such menial tasks as carrying water and collecting firewood. Although the Mi'kmaq and the French each believed that they were the superior people, they usually lived together in peace because each had something the other wanted.

The fur trade was probably the most important reason for this peace. The Mi'kmaq exchanged beaver pelts and bear and moose hides for French guns, copper kettles and iron tools. These manufactured goods cost the European traders very little, whereas the furs were worth a lot of money in Europe. The French traders believed that they profited more from this trade. The Mi'kmaq, in turn, believed that they had made the better deal. In exchange for goods that they could not obtain elsewhere, the Mi'kmaq often traded the clothes off their backs. French hat makers preferred these used pelts to freshly skinned furs because the animal grease the Mi'kmaq smeared on their bodies made the furs more pliable.

The Mi'kmaq traded to make their lives easier. Iron knives and axes were stronger and remained sharp longer than stone or bone tools. Muskets were better than arrows because they could kill from a greater distance. Copper kettles were more durable than wood or stone cooking vessels. It was easier to trade for cloth than to make clothes from hides. Glass beads, brandy, tobacco, beans, flour, biscuits, iron harpoons, metal fish hooks and blankets were also desirable trade items. In addition to furs, the Mi'kmaq traded their handicrafts to the French. Mi'kmaq wood, bone and stone carvings were valued in Europe. Pieces of birchbark were embroidered with moose hair or covered with porcupine-quill designs and sold as souvenirs. Gradually, the Mi'kmaq women began to incorporate European techniques and materials in their artwork.

These trading partners soon became military allies; in fact, the word "Mi'kmaq" means "ally." The Mi'kmaq acted as scouts for the French soldiers, raided British settlements and captured British ships in the harbour. However, they always remained independent and decided for themselves when to fight and when to hide or retreat. The Europeans considered the Mi'kmaq's refusal to stay and fight in a losing cause to be cowardly, whereas the Mi'kmaq believed the Europeans' obedience to authority, even in the face of certain death, to be the greatest of follies.

When the first colonists came to Acadia, the Mi'kmaq were generous and willingly shared their belongings with the strangers. The colonists had no idea what was safe to eat. They did not know where to settle, how to travel over the deep snow or where to cross the swiftly flowing rivers. The Mi'kmaq acted as guides. They taught the Acadians how to use canoes, toboggans, snowshoes and moccasins, and how to hunt and where to fish. When the settlers ran out of food, the Mi'kmaq fed them. When they became sick, the Mi'kmaq showed them which roots and herbs would cure them. Many of the first explorers and settlers suffered and even died from scurvy, which is caused by a lack of vitamin C. The Mi'kmaq taught them how to make a broth from the needles and bark of the white cedar tree to prevent this disease.

Because there were so few Europeans in Acadia, the Mi'kmaq continued to hunt and fish as they wished. When Great Britain won control of Nova Scotia, France tried to convince the Mi'kmaq there to relocate to Cape Breton or even to Prince Edward Island, but they refused. It was lack of power, rather than lack of desire, that prevented the French from attempting to control the Mi'kmaq. The priests had the most influence over the Mi'kmaq. To "civilize" and convert the Mi'kmaq, the priests attempted to convince them to give up their nomadic ways and to adopt agricultural pursuits. In the early 1730s, two French Abbés, Gaulin and Courtin, established a settlement at Malpeque for the Île St. Jean Mi'kmaq. The Mi'kmaq, however, were not interested in forsaking their old way of life, and since the priest visited them only once a year, the mission was never very successful. The French had the most extensive contact with the Mi'kmaq during the festivities of Saint Anne's Day (Saint Anne was the Mi'kmaq patron saint) and the annual summer visit of the governor of Île Royale to Port LaJoye to distribute presents. The French authorities took advantage of these meetings to gather information about the activities of the English colonists from Nova Scotia, to gain the Mi'kmaq's goodwill and to incite them against the British.

Trading partners

As the number of Acadian settlers grew, the Mi'kmaq began to face serious problems. Perhaps the worst of these was disease. Europeans brought with them such diseases as smallpox, influenza, chicken pox, whooping cough, tuberculosis, syphilis and scarlet fever. As the Mi'kmaq had never been exposed to these diseases, their bodies had not built up immunity to them, and even measles could be deadly. The Mi'kmaq's growing dependence on alcohol and unfamiliar European food weakened their resistance to certain diseases, and they died by the thousands. One estimate places the number at ten Mi'kmaq dead for every one who survived.

The shamans, who were the communities' doctors as well as their spiritual leaders, could not cure these new diseases, and the Mi'kmaq began to doubt their shamans' power. This made it easier for the French missionaries to convert the Mi'kmaq to Christianity. When animals became items of trade rather than life-giving food, the spiritual bond that had once united the hunter and his prey disintegrated, and the Mi'kmaq began to adopt a more materialistic attitude towards their environment. Energy spent hunting and trapping for furs to trade was time away from traditional pursuits. The Mi'kmaq soon became torn between loyalty to their own spiritual beliefs and the religious ideas of the Catholic priests. Their culture was being slowly undermined.

Another blow to Mi'kmaq culture was the introduction of alcohol as a trade item. Despite the complaints of the Catholic priests, the Europeans traded brandy with the Mi'kmaq. The Mi'kmaq were not accustomed to alcohol, which had a detrimental effect on them. Some researchers suggest that this was due to a slightly different body chemistry from that of the Europeans. Other academics explain the Mi'kmaq's tendency to become drunk on their religious beliefs, which emphasized achieving a trance-like state before communing with the spirits.

By 1758, the Mi'kmaq had become reliant upon the fur traders for most of their food, clothes and tools. To obtain these goods, the Mi'kmaq had to bring in animal hides and pelts. As the demand for furs increased, more animals were killed, and the amount of game steadily declined. Thus, when the European traders deserted their fur-trading posts in the Maritime region for the more profitable beaver lands in western Canada, the Mi'kmaq were no longer able to feed and clothe themselves as they had done in the past. The "good old days" had disappeared. The arrival of the Europeans had changed the Mi'kmaq's way of life. Soon there were more Acadian settlers than Mi'kmaq, and the Mi'kmaq became dependent upon them for survival.

The Acadians

By the middle of the eighteenth century, Great Britain was becoming more and more worried about the Acadians still living in Nova Scotia. The British distrusted them because they were Roman Catholics, spoke French and listened to their French-born priests. Five times since 1713 the British governors of Acadia had attempted to persuade the Acadians to swear an oath of allegiance to the British monarch, and each time the Acadians had refused.

Finally, in 1755, the British governor of Nova Scotia, Charles Lawrence, ordered the Acadians to sign an oath of loyalty to Great Britain or be deported from the colony. The Acadians didn't want to fight for either Great Britain or France: they considered themselves neither French nor British, but Acadians. In the past they had remained neutral, and they promised to remain neutral in all future wars. Lawrence, however, did not believe the Acadians and ordered their deportation. Thousands of settlers were rounded up, herded onto ships and sent to other British colonies. To escape this fate, some two thousand Acadians fled to Île St. Jean.

This exodus brought total confusion to Île St. Jean. In less than three years the population almost tripled. In the previous five years there had been only one good crop on the Island, so food was scarce. Many of the newcomers had arrived with only the clothes they were wearing, and families wandered from barn to barn seeking food and shelter. Life was miserable, but the Acadians believed that even this life was preferable to being deported to a strange land.

In 1756, Great Britain and France were again at war in Europe, and once more, the fighting spilled over into North America. Many of the young men on Île St. Jean went to Louisbourg to help defend the fortress, but in July 1758, Louisbourg surrendered to the British fleet. Lord Rollo, one of the British commanders, then sailed to Île St. Jean with four warships. His orders were to remove all the

The expulsion of the Acadians

Acadians, build a fort on the Island, destroy the crops and kill the livestock. The purpose of the last two orders was to discourage the Acadians from returning.

Lord Rollo sailed into Hillsborough Bay on August 17, 1758. The Acadians, having only a few cannons and muskets, had no chance of victory. When the inhabitants of Port LaJoye saw Lord Rollo's ships approaching, the women and children hid in the forest and buried their personal belongings and religious ornaments. The more daring inhabitants made their way to the north shore, and with the help of the Mi'kmaq, escaped to New France or to the

The Original Acadians

Approximately nine out of every ten Acadians on Prince Edward Island today are descended from the families listed in this chart. These families, listed in the 1798 census, were among those who avoided capture by the British in 1758:

Arsenault	Doiron	Longueepee
Aucoin	Doucet	Martin
Bernard	Downing	Michel
Blanchard	Gallant	Muise
Blaquiere	Gaudet	Pineau
Bourque	Gauthier	Pitre
Buote	Gautreau	Poirier
Cheverie	Landry	Richard
Chiasson	Le Brun	Roussel
Des Roches	Le Clerc	St-Jean

Some Acadians later Anglicized their names: Aucoin became Wedge, Poirier became Perry, Pitre became Peters, LeClerc became Le Clair and Bourque became Burke.

French islands of St. Pierre and Miquelon off the coast of Newfoundland. The garrison at Port LaJoye surrendered without firing a shot.

The British soldiers eventually caught most of the Acadians and herded them to Port LaJoye. These prisoners, who had not fought in the war, begged to remain on the Island, but the British ignored their pleas and shipped about three thousand dispirited Acadians to Louisbourg. There they were allowed to pack only their clothes and a few personal belongings. Animals, tools, dishes and the rest of their possessions were left behind for the conquerors. From Louisbourg, the Acadians were crowded aboard ships and sent to France. Approximately seven hundred Acadians who embarked on the *Duke William* and the *Violet* perished at sea in December 1758. A violent Atlantic storm damaged both ships. Before the men on board the *Duke William* could aid their sister vessel, another squall separated the two ships and all four hundred of the *Violet's* passengers were drowned. A similar fate awaited the *Duke William*, which began taking on more water than the men, including the Acadians, could pump out. The captain distributed the remaining liquor to the people, and kept the ship afloat by filling casks with air and placing them below deck. Twice, vessels approached the stricken ship only to sail away. When all seemed lost, the Acadians apparently requested that their captors take the lifeboats and leave them aboard, there not being enough boats for everyone. Reluctantly, the captain agreed. Just before the *Duke William* sank, four Acadians discovered a small boat and escaped. "The *Duke William* [according to their report] swam till it felt calm, and as she went down her decks blew up. The noise was like the explosion of a gun, or a loud clap of thunder."

We can only imagine the feelings of those Acadians who arrived safely in France, most of them for the first time. For years they had struggled in Acadia to clear the forests, plant crops and build homes. Now all their hard work was in the hands of the hated British. The Acadians would have to begin a new life in a strange land.

During the next twenty-five years, some Acadians returned to Acadia. Others remained where they had been deported in the West Indies, the United States (some becoming the Cajuns of Louisiana) and as far away as the Falkland Islands. Approximately thirty families near Malpeque managed to stay hidden from Lord Rollo's troops. Most of the present Acadian population of Prince Edward Island is descended from these families, or from deported Acadians who later returned.

On October 7, 1763, the war between Great Britain and France officially ended. North America became a British possession, and Île St. Jean was renamed St. John's Island. At Fort Amherst, which was built on the site of Port LaJoye, the British flag was raised on Island soil. France's control of the Island had ended.

FOUR

King George III

The Arrival of the British

Great Britain now owned St. John's Island. The problem was deciding what to do with it. There was good fishing in the area, but how valuable were its other resources? No one knew the answers to this question, but many people in Great Britain were willing to gamble that the Island was valuable. In 1763, with the ink barely dry on the peace treaty, King George III was flooded with requests for land. One individual, Lord Egmont, even asked the King to give him the whole of St. John's Island.

Dividing Up the Land

George III decided to learn more about his new colonies in North America before making any decisions, and in 1764 he hired Captain Samuel Jan Holland to survey St. John's Island, Cape Breton and the Magdalens (a group of islands in the Gulf of St. Lawrence). Captain Holland, a military engineer and a skilled cartographer, was well suited to the task. He had fought with the British soldiers when they had captured Louisbourg in 1758, and he was anxious to see Great Britain settle the conquered lands. The following is a paraphrase of Captain Holland's description of his work on St. John's Island:

> We arrived at Hillsborough Bay in the fall of 1764. Fortunately, I had been warned to bring extra food and building materials, because there was no place for us to stay. Fort Amherst, which was built by Lord Rollo, is falling down. My men immediately built a house near the seashore at Rocky Point from the ruins of some old houses. It is a good spot to chart the stars, but it is not very comfortable.

I wished to start surveying as soon as possible, but the naval commander refused use of some of his equipment, and then Marie Josephte bore me a handsome son. I wouldn't be surprised if John Frederick wasn't the first British baby born on St. John's Island. When we were finally able to work, it was winter. The weather was so cold that one soldier froze to death and several others suffered from frost-bitten hands and feet.

I divided the men into small groups of five people. Each field group loaded their toboggans with warm coats, blankets, and food and drink for eight days. I hired some Acadians to guide us, and we used their dogs to pull the toboggans. I feel sorry for the Acadians. They are treated like enemy prisoners by the soldiers, and they are very poor ...

The most difficult problem was deciding which location would make the best capital. The choice was between the villages I have named Charlottetown, Georgetown and Princetown. All have excellent harbours — which is very important for transportation and defence. Princetown has the best location for fishing. Georgetown's three rivers provide excellent routes inland. I finally chose Charlottetown. It is near the middle of the Island and its three rivers provide easy travel into the interior. A small stream runs through Charlottetown and provides pure drinking water. The site is also easily defended. The cannons at Fort Amherst control the harbour. If enemy troops do land, they must cross one of the two rivers before attacking the capital. In addition, Charlottetown is closest to the mainland and is thus best suited for trading with Nova Scotia and Quebec.

Captain S. J. Holland, 1765

Holland finished his survey and moved on to the Magdalens. Although his map was drawn up without any consideration of the current inhabitants and contained a number of mistakes, the survey formed the basis of the present division of land. He divided the Island into 67 lots or townships of about 8,000 hectares (20,000 acres) each, three counties (Kings, Queens and Prince), 14 parishes, and three "royalties" set aside for the pastures and garden plots of Georgetown, Charlottetown and Princetown residents.

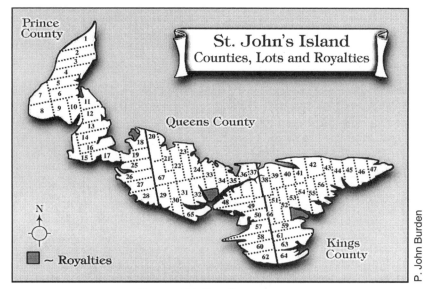

P. John Burden

Samuel Holland's survey

After the survey was completed, the British government was still not certain what to do with St. John's Island, and it was being deluged with requests for large parcels of the Island from many wealthy and important people. Every applicant was interviewed and told to write a letter explaining why he deserved the land. The government then selected about one hundred people to take part in a lottery.

On July 23, 1767, nearly the entire Island was given away. The land was chosen by lot. Each person's name was written on a slip of paper and placed in a box. The first name picked (Philip Stevens) received township number one; the second name chosen received township number two. This continued until all sixty-seven townships had been granted. The King kept Township 66, and reserved additional land for schools, churches and for the county capitals Georgetown, Charlottetown and Princetown (now called Summerside). Lots 40 and 59 had been granted prior to the lottery.

The British government required the new owners to settle the land, pay for the construction of roads and jails and provide salaries for judges, sheriffs and government leaders. Each landlord also had to pay a small annual fee, called a quit rent, for his land. The more valuable the land, the higher the quit rent. The owners were also obligated to settle, within ten years, one Protestant person (but not from Great Britain so as not to deplete the country's population) for every 44.5 hectares (110 acres) they had been allotted. Roman Catholics were not wanted as settlers because the British distrusted them — especially after the recent wars with Catholic France. If these terms were not fulfilled, the government reserved the right to repossess the land.

Very few owners, however, either paid their quit rents to the government or brought over settlers. Many had asked for the land solely to make money through speculation. After ten years, one-quarter of the lots had been sold at least once, but few settlers had been brought to the Island.

Although most of the landlords lost interest in the Island, several attempted to colonize their lands. Sir James Montgomery founded settlements at Covehead and Stanhope. Robert Stewart sent Scottish settlers to Malpeque. Captain John MacDonald established colonies at Tracadie and Scotchfort. Robert Clark brought colonists to New London. Captain Holland sponsored a few families at Cape Traverse. Thomas Des Brisay sent nine families to Lots 31 and 33. From 1770 to 1775, almost 1,000 people came to Prince Edward Island. Although the landlords' leases required that only Protestants be settled on the Island, the majority of the immigrants were Scottish Roman Catholics. The rest were mostly English and Scottish Protestants. By 1783, nineteen of the sixty-seven lots had been settled, and there were 1,200 settlers on the Island, not including several hundred Acadians and Mi'kmaq.

Arrival In a Strange Land

It is hard to imagine the difficulties and problems faced by the first immigrants to Prince Edward Island. The voyage across the Atlantic often tested the endurance of the hardiest passengers. Crowded together below deck for up to two months, with stale water and little food, the passengers often became sick and died. Some vessels sailed peacefully across the Atlantic, while others had nothing but trouble. The *Falmouth*, the *Annabella*, the *Alexander* and the *Elizabeth* were four such ships. Thomas Curtis sailed to Prince Edward Island in 1775 aboard the latter vessel, and upon returning to England wrote a long account of his experiences. The following is a paraphrased account of his travels:

In 1775 I was a young man in London, England, looking for a way to make a quick fortune. One day, I learned that Robert Clark was planning to take settlers to St. John's Island and went to visit him. His stories about the Island convinced me to travel to this glorious land. The rivers were filled with fish. There were so many deer and turkeys, he said, you shot them through the window. It all sounded good. You could have offered me 500 pounds to stay in London and I would have refused.

The Elizabeth set sail on August 18, 1775. For three days I was so seasick I didn't leave my bed. For those of us who could not afford rooms on deck, it was very disagreeable. Candles provided our light, pails our washroom, and salt water our bathwater.

After a week or two, our appetites returned. But salted beef and pork, with pudding twice a week, was not my idea of living. It was about this time that we began to drink our sorrows away. There was nothing to do all day but watch the sky and the waves. One day we gave some rum to the sailors. We regretted this afterwards because if the storm had come twelve hours earlier, we would all have been drowned. I mention this as a warning to others.

Several weeks later we sighted Newfoundland. The weather turned very cold. Porpoises surrounded our vessel until we fired several shots at them. That evening we caught our first fish — cod and halibut. They were cooked in a large iron pot with slices of pork fat. The dish is called chowder. It burnt in the pot, but having had nothing fresh for many weeks, most of us ate so much we were sick afterwards.

On the fifth of November, one of the men on deck cried out "land on the lee bow." The wind was blowing hard and we all feared for our lives as the gale blew us towards shore. The anchors were dropped, but still we drifted closer to the sand banks. The captain ordered the masts cut down. Nothing worked! We could see the terrible breakers we must pass through to arrive safely on shore. The damaged ship drifted over four sand bars before running aground.

The lifeboats were brought out. But no one wished to go first for fear the beach was quicksand. Finally, one brave man volunteered. In a few hours we were all safe on shore. A fire was started to warm our limbs, and we gave thanks to God.

We had nothing; no chair, no table, no bed, no food and no shelter. All that touched my lips for three days were a few cranberries, wet tobacco and salt water. What the others had in their pockets I didn't know, but I did not hear of anyone having more than a few soggy biscuits.

That first evening we decided to gather wood to make a shelter. As we had nothing but pocket knives, the shelter leaked and we spent the night huddled before the fire. I had come ashore with my warm cork jacket and did not take it off night or day. No money in the world could have bought it from me.

The second night the storm blew our house down. It then began to snow. By the morning, everyone was complaining of hunger. I imagined such horrible scenes as eating our dog, or throwing dice to see which one of us would be eaten first. The next morning, however, the wind died down, and we paddled out to the ship. The casks of oatmeal were soggy and full of sand, but everyone was so hungry that we dipped our heads into the barrels. We ate more like pigs than men. Later, the women cooked oatmeal cakes. Although they were burnt on the outside and raw in the middle, the cakes were the sweetest thing I had ever eaten in my life.

For the next week we worked constantly to rescue the clothing and equipment from the vessel. We were constantly wet. When the exhausted men lay down to sleep by the fire, two men kept watch to keep their feet from getting too close to the flames. On the ninth day a boat arrived. We were saved!

Thomas Curtis' experiences were worse than most of the pioneers, and he returned to England as soon as he could. The final words in his diary were: "I can not express the joy I felt when I arrived home, the 2nd of February, 1777."

Vanguards of Settlement

Many of the early settlers to Prince Edward Island came in groups under the auspices of one of the large landowners. The following section describes the mixed results of the settlement schemes of James Montgomery, Captain John MacDonald and the Earl of Selkirk.

James Montgomery was one of the most important politicians and businessmen in Scotland. In 1769 he became interested in establishing a flax farm on P.E.I. and soon gained control of almost 40,470 hectares (99,960 acres) of land. He hired David Lawson, a Scottish flax farmer, to manage this farm. The farm work was to be performed by fifty servants, who agreed to serve for four years, after which time Montgomery promised to rent them land at inexpensive rates.

The Scottish settlers arrived at Stanhope Cove in June 1770. They faced many problems. Stanhope was a complete wilderness. There were no people or buildings, and the only nourishment available was oatmeal, berries and seafood. A shipload of food finally arrived, but the horses and farm equipment never did come. Because there were no farm implements available on the Island, the settlers had to make all their own tools.

Slowly the colonists cleared the land, planted seeds and built a water mill to grind grain. Two years later, the mill was destroyed by fire. Lawson rebuilt the mill, but the very day it was completed, it burned down again. On the third attempt, the land around the mill was protected from fire. A short time later, the mill dam was destroyed by a flood. Lawson also had problems with his workers. In the first year, one man was crushed when a large pine tree he was chopping fell on him. Two other men drowned. Finally, just when the flax farm began to make money, the servants' contracts expired and they scattered across the Island.

Montgomery became worried about the lack of profits and wrote Lawson for an explanation. However, the American Revolution had begun, and Montgomery was unable to correspond with Lawson for six years. The war also stopped all immigration to the Island. Montgomery finally contacted his farm manager and dismissed him. Montgomery had lost faith in the Island and now turned his attention elsewhere.

Captain John MacDonald's reasons for settling the Tracadie area (Lot 36) in 1772 were quite different from Montgomery's motives for colonizing Stanhope. The Roman Catholic Church in Scotland had asked Captain MacDonald to transport Catholic tenant farmers to North America. Catholicism had been illegal in Scotland for more than one hundred and fifty years, but it had managed to survive in the isolated Scottish Highlands. Several uprisings against the British king, however, had convinced the British government to take severe measures against the Highland Catholics. For example, the owner of South Uist Island in the Hebrides decided to convert the Catholics on his property to Protestantism. A Protestant teacher was hired to proselytize the children, who were forced to eat meat during Lent and to copy anti-Catholic sentences in their writing books. When other islands in the Hebrides began to adopt these practices, the Catholic bishops became alarmed and sought a way to end this religious persecution.

The Scottish Protestant landowners in the Hebrides had a serious weakness. To prosper they needed a large number of tenants to farm their extensive, rocky lands. The Catholic Church, therefore, decided to force the owners to grant better conditions by threatening to transport the tenants to North America. The Bishops turned to MacDonald to organize such an expedition.

Captain John, as he was later called on Prince Edward Island, was a proud and fearless Highland Scot whose hot temper and critical statements often created enemies. On one occasion, he was challenged to a duel. He was well educated and could speak seven languages. A devout Roman Catholic, he wished to help his fellow Catholics and preserve Scottish culture and ideas in the New World.

John MacDonald sent his brother Donald to America in search of a suitable place to establish a colony. Favourable rumours about the flax farm started by Sir James Montgomery at his settlement in the Tracadie area, as well as exaggerated stories about the rich soil and mild climate, convinced the Catholic bishops to follow through with their plans to send some of their flock to the Island. MacDonald bought Lot 36 from Montgomery and began to recruit settlers.

American Raiders and the Loyalists

Provisions were scarce in these early years of British settlement. Only a few villages were self-sufficient. The rest relied on Great Britain for supplies. In the same month that the *Elizabeth* landed on the north shore, two American warships appeared in Charlottetown harbour. The Thirteen Colonies had just declared their independence from Great Britain, and several American privateers were taking advantage of the situation to loot British towns in North America. The acting governor, Phillips Callbeck, wrote the following paraphrased account of this raid:

> *We had no soldiers to defend the town ... Despite my kind words, the American captain ordered me aboard his ship. One of the sailors hit me in the face. The invaders then began to loot the town. They broke into the warehouses and stole the food and supplies intended for the settlers. Next, they smashed their way into my house ... Not satisfied with this, these evil men drank our wine. Then they began to hunt for my wife to "cut her throat." This was because her father was living in the United States and was loyal to Britain. Fortunately, Elizabeth was at our farm in the country. These brutal men left us without a single glass of wine, without a candle to burn, bread to eat, nor clothes to wear.*

> *After this cruelty, Mr. Wright, a prominent Charlotte Town citizen, was also captured. The rebels swore and laughed at the tears of his wife and sister. Finally, they sailed away. Mr. Wright and I were forced to go with them.*

The affair ended happily for Callbeck and Wright. When the ship landed in Boston, George Washington apologized for their rude treatment and set them free. New London was not as lucky, as the plundered provisions had been intended for the settlers there.

Following the American Revolution (1775-1783), many people decided to leave the newly independent United States for British territory. Roughly six hundred of these "Loyalists" came to settle in Bedeque, Orwell, Tryon, Vernon River and East Point; however, several hundred of them left the Island when they discovered that they could not buy land. Most landlords would rent to the Loyalists, but as with the other immigrants, would not sell them land. Those Loyalists who did remain contributed their skills to the colony's development.

The Protestant landowners in the Hebrides did not want their tenants to leave, and they spread rumours that anyone who went to the Island would be sold into slavery. Partly as a result of these rumours, only 210 people agreed to leave for the Island in 1772. Captain John remained in Scotland to look after the finances and recruit more people. His brother, who had gone ahead with seventeen families to Scotchfort (Lot 36) the previous year, was put in charge of the settlement. The threat to remove all the Catholic tenant farmers from the Hebrides had the desired result. To prevent more Highland settlers from leaving, Protestant landowners lowered their rents and promised to allow freedom of religion.

The settlers who arrived in Scotchfort were unhappy with the wilderness conditions they found. Some talked about moving to Nova Scotia, where they could own their own farms since the land was not held by absentee landowners. A Catholic priest wrote, "There is no money, no clothes, and no meat unless we pay four times what it is worth. It breaks my heart that my poor friends who were doing well before they left Scotland are now upon the brink of great misery and poverty."

The following year, Captain John arrived with more colonists and supplies of grain and food. The colony survived. As a landlord, Captain John encouraged his tenants to continue their traditional farming methods. Although this policy helped to preserve Highland culture on the Island, raising livestock was not the most profitable farming activity. MacDonald also kept the best land for his family and refused to rent or sell it to his tenants. More Scottish settlers soon followed. The largest group of these came under the auspices of Thomas Douglas, Earl of Selkirk.

Thomas Douglas had not expected to be in a position of influence; however, his four older brothers had all died, and he had inherited enough money to carry out his dreams. Despite poor health, Selkirk was a bundle of nervous energy. He could never sit still and was always busy planning projects. The three adjectives that best describe his personality are impetuous, stubborn and ambitious. Selkirk would often commit to a project before he had carefully thought it out. Yet once he decided on something, he kept at it until it was finished.

In 1802, Selkirk decided to establish a colony in the New World. The decision to settle Highland Scots on Prince Edward Island was the result of a series of accidents, rather than a deliberate choice. Initially, he had wanted to transport poor Irishmen to Louisiana, but this plan failed. He then turned his attention to Highlanders. The Scots were an obvious choice as potential settlers: unemployment was high in Scotland, and the crops had failed several years in a row. Scottish tenant farmers were being forced off their lands and replaced by a far smaller number of sheep ranchers. Selkirk did most of his recruiting in the Hebrides, particularly on the Isle of Skye.

First, Selkirk considered shipping the Highlanders to the United States. When the British government objected to this plan, he decided upon Upper Canada (present-day Ontario) instead. Then, only weeks before the Scottish families were to leave, the British government withdrew its offer of free land in Upper Canada. After a week of furious dealings, Selkirk bought 32,370 hectares (79,953 acres) on Prince Edward Island. Early in the summer of 1803, about eight hundred Highlanders set sail for the Orwell-Point Prim area aboard the *Polly,* the *Dykes* and the *Oughton.*

Even though the Selkirk settlers experienced the same problems that had plagued earlier immigrants, the settlement prospered. One of the reasons for this success was that Selkirk felt responsible for his settlers and tried to help them get established. Instead of encouraging the colonists to spread out, he kept them together so they could preserve old values and customs and help one another. Selkirk did this by dividing the land into long, narrow strips extending to the shore, so the distance between families was seldom more than 1.6 kilometres (1 mile). Selkirk also lifted the people's spirits by selling rather than renting the land: the settlers knew that if they worked hard, they would be able to buy their own farms. Equally important, the Highlanders who came with Selkirk had been among the most prosperous tenant farmers in Scotland. They came to the Island because they wished to. Such people were more likely to do well than poor tenant farmers who had been forced to leave Scotland.

Selkirk remained only a few months on the Island, and his subsequent contacts with the Island were not satisfactory. His agent on the Island did not keep him informed about the colony's progress and sold the valuable timber on his property without

Selkirk's approval. Selkirk gradually lost interest in the Island and turned his attention to establishing the Red River colony near present-day Winnipeg. His legacy on the Island, however, remained. The colonists had arrived.

FIVE

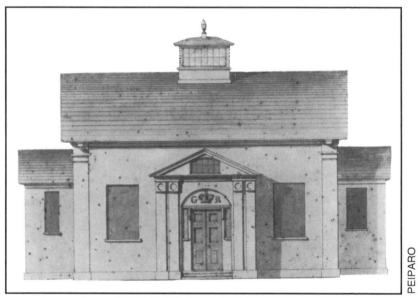

Architect's drawing of Charlottetown's
Courts of Justice and Houses of Assembly

PEIPARO

Early Island
Government

Following the British conquest in 1758, the Island was governed by the authorities in Nova Scotia. In 1769, St. John's Island was separated politically from Nova Scotia, and the British government appointed a governor to look after the Island's affairs. The governor was the most important politician in the colony, and appointed most of the judges, sheriffs and military officers. He was leader of the armed forces on the Island, and every law required his signature.

The first governor was Captain Walter Patterson, a native of Ireland. He was probably quite shocked when he first stepped ashore in Charlottetown in 1770, as there were only two decent buildings and a few log huts in the entire town, even though it was the capital of the Island. There was no courthouse, no jail and no place of worship. The population numbered little more than three hundred and most of the people were Acadians. Although the Acadians were no longer in danger of deportation, their loyalty was suspect. They had promised to be loyal, but they hadn't had much of a choice. Those Acadians who refused to pledge their loyalty were not allowed to remain on the Island nor to fish near it.

Patterson was energetic, intelligent and hardworking. Although he wasn't always diplomatic, he appeared to have had the Island's best interests at heart. "St. John's Island is my child," he wrote. "I have fostered it at the expense of my fortune and a great part of the prime of my life." His oldest son was called William *St. John* Patterson, after "his" Island.

For the first few months after his appointment, Governor Patterson was kept busy just attending to his own everyday needs. A house was built to keep out the approaching cold. Since there was no extra food available on the Island, the governor bought his winter's supply of food as well clothing from Nova Scotia before the

Northumberland Strait froze. Captain Patterson was expecting more officials to come to the Island that year, but the conditions were so bad in Charlottetown that he warned them not to come until later. "There is not a house to put your head into," he moaned, "and if you do not bring food and other goods to last until June, you will starve because there is not a loaf of bread, or the flour to make a loaf, to be bought on the Island."

Patterson's most important task was to establish a government for the Island. The British government had instructed Patterson to choose twelve men to aid him in drawing up laws, but Patterson could find no more than seven qualified people. These seven

Early Laws

The first laws dealt with such issues as building roads and bridges, hunting walruses and preventing crimes.

Like settlers elsewhere in North America, the population of St. John's Island declared war on the larger wildlife in the wilderness around them:

A reward of fifteen shillings shall be given to every person who shall kill a bear and bring in its snout as proof. A sum of five shillings shall be paid to anyone who shall bring in the snout of a lynx.

In 1781, a debate arose on the Island about the slaves who had been brought to the colony. Some people argued that all slaves who became Christians should be set free; others disagreed. The following law was passed by the Assembly:

1. All slaves, whether Negro or half-black, shall remain as slaves whether they convert to Christianity or not.

2. Slaves may only be freed by their owners.

3. The children of female slaves shall belong to their mother's master.

Minor crimes were punished by a public whipping, or the criminal was placed in a pillory for everyone to see. Theft after dark was a capital crime. In Charlottetown, the hanging hill on Euston Street between Prince Street and Malpeque Road (now called University Avenue) always attracted a large crowd. One time, however, the sheriff was unable to persuade anyone to act as the public executioner to hang a woman accused of stealing, and she was freed.

formed the Council, and its job was to advise the governor. Unfortunately, most of the councillors had been trained as soldiers and knew very little about government.

As the population continued to grow, the British government decided to give Island men a voice in their own government by creating an elected Assembly. Voting regulations gave the vote to male Protestants over twenty-one years of age, and until 1853, property qualifications disenfranchised most squatters and labourers. In 1773, the first elections were held, and eighteen men were elected to help the governor and his council make laws. Although the Assembly did not become very powerful until the 1850s, it gave the people a chance to inform the governor of their opinions and needs. The governor, however, did not have to carry out the Assembly's wishes, and because St. John's Island was a British colony, no bill could become law until it was approved by the British government.

The most pressing problem was the landlords' continuing refusal to pay their quit rents. The quit rent money was needed to pay the governor's salary, erect public buildings and help run the government. The lack of funds was partly solved in 1777, when Patterson convinced the British government to pay the costs of governing the Island. However, the problem of collecting quit rents remained.

Elections

In the early days of the settlement, elections were usually wild affairs. Until 1787, everyone had to travel to Charlottetown to vote. The polls stayed open several days to allow distant settlers time to vote, and to enable people to cast their ballots in every constituency in which they held property. The people voted by raising their hands or by yelling out which candidates they wanted to represent them in the government. Voting tended to take place in blocks, as each candidate's supporters took turns controlling the hustings. Since voting was not a secret, it was easier to bribe voters. Candidates sometimes offered free liquor to everyone who promised to vote for them, and fights occasionally broke out among supporters of different candidates. Only much later did the secret ballot and laws against drinking on election days end the violence.

The most infamous election brawl took place in 1847 near Belfast, an area that consisted of Loyalists, Scottish Protestants, and a minority of Irish Roman Catholics. Election violence the previous year had caused many people to question the results, and the government had called a by-election for March 1. Ethnic, religious and class tensions, however, remained high, and in two separate incidents during the election, mobs of Irish and Scottish tenants attacked each other with clubs, fists and feet. When the electoral officials attempted to assist the victims, they also were beaten. At least three people were killed and the blood of many others stained the freshly fallen snow.

The Great Land Swindle

Many government officials appointed by Great Britain came from Great Britain to the Island hoping to make a fortune; however, very few government jobs paid well. One way the officials could make money was to obtain land. Governor Patterson's desire to own more land on the Island led to his downfall.

In 1781, Patterson decided to sell the land of some landlords who had not paid their quit rents. Eleven townships were sold at a public auction, but the date of the auction had been kept secret. Only Patterson and a few of his friends attended it. The governor personally bought 40,470 hectares (99,960 acres) at a ridiculously low price.

This auction created a storm. The landlords initiated a campaign in London to have Patterson removed. They complained to the British government that they had not been informed of the sale, and also argued that the governor had taken the best land on the Island, and that he had sold the land belonging to many of those people whom he disliked.

The powerful Stewart and Des Brisay families were particularly angered by the auction. Patterson had left them only a few lots. Their dislike of the governor grew to hatred when it was revealed that Patterson had stolen the heart of Peter Stewart's wife while her husband had been sick in bed with rheumatism, and the two families petitioned the British government to remove the governor.

In 1786, Governor Walter Patterson was ordered to return to England, but he refused to comply for another three years. When Patterson finally arrived, he was bankrupt. His property on St. John's Island had been sold by his enemies for much less than it was worth, and the British government would not offer him another post. Walter Patterson, the Island's first governor, died in London in 1798, in poverty and disgrace.

Another Name Change for the Island

Prince Edward Island has had many names, from the Mi'kmaq *Abegweit* or *Minegoo*, to the French *Île St. Jean*, to the British *St. John's Island*.

In 1780, the Island government pointed out that there were at least eight ports, rivers and forts named St. John in the Atlantic colonies. Since the Island was often confused with these locales, and mail was frequently sent to the wrong place, the legislature had renamed the Island "New Ireland." This name had probably been selected by Governor Patterson, who was a native of Ireland, but the British government refused to accept it, arguing that "New Ireland" had already been taken by another colony. "You may," it wrote, "change the name to *New Guernsey* or *New Anglese*." These two suggestions were turned down by the Island government.

Finally, in 1799, the colony was officially named Prince Edward Island in honour of the son of King George III. Prince Edward had never visited the colony, but he had ordered that its defences be improved, and this is one reason the Island's government selected his name. What the people weren't aware of was that the prince had suggested that the government of St. John's Island be joined with the government of Nova Scotia. If this fact had been known, the province probably would not have its present name.

SIX

Women gathered for a hooking and spinning frolic

PEIPARO

Pioneer Life

Most British immigrants were not prepared for the Island wilderness. The land had to be cleared of trees, stumps and rocks; homes had to be built and crops planted before winter; and virtually no one on the Island could advise them. Progress was agonizingly slow. The British government generally ignored Prince Edward Island in favour of its other North American possessions. The Island lacked rich mineral deposits and, by treaty, the Americans controlled the Gulf fishery. Farmland was inferior to many other areas in British North America, and few settlers wished to rent land on the Island when they could purchase their own farms quite cheaply in other British colonies. As a result, the Island generally attracted only the poorer and less-educated immigrants.

The population increased slowly, and more land was cleared. By 1800, Prince Edward Island had become self-sufficient in food and had even begun to export small surpluses. Twenty years later, the population had grown to about fifteen thousand people. By the 1830s, the settlers had developed a sense of community and local pride. As one visitor to the Island wrote in 1834, "Verily, this is a good poor man's country!"

The Acadians had a particularly difficult row to hoe. Those who had escaped deportation in 1758 lived for several years in fear of being forcibly removed from the Island. They supported themselves by hunting and fishing. Occasionally, British merchants hired them as fishers or boat builders, and paid them with clothing, rum, flour or ammunition. As the numbers of British immigrants increased, the Acadians were forced to give up the land they had cleared and travel elsewhere. Some families moved several times. No sooner had they cleared the land than they were evicted by the landlord. Eventually the Acadians made their way to Egmont Bay, Tignish, Miscouche,

Mont Carmel, Cascumpeque, Rollo Bay and Bloomfield. Roman Catholics in general were second-class citizens on the Island. Whether of Acadian, Scottish or Irish descent they were not legally allowed to own land until 1786, and they were denied the vote until 1830.

Acadian Ballad

The first two verses in this ballad by Julitte Arsenault describe the departure of one group of Acadians from Malpeque to Egmont Bay:

Who were the ones who drove us here?
Twas the wicked people in our land.
A whole crew they were.
Agin the Acadians
And all together
Living off our goods.

Scarcely do we pick a grain of wheat
When we have to run to them with it.
Those barbarians
Without charity
Care not one bit
For our poverty.

Since there were so few Acadians on the Island and each community was remote from the others, Acadian settlements tended to become inbred. As one missionary wrote to his superior in 1800: "I cannot disapprove of the aversion they have for marrying their neighbours because it has meant that they have kept their faith, their customs, and their piety intact." Despite being isolated from each other, the Acadian communities clung to their traditions and resisted assimilation. They lived apart from the other inhabitants and retained their traditional dress, which further isolated them.

Other ethnic groups also tended to settle in their own small, insular coastal communities. The Scots were the largest single group, but they were divided among themselves by religion and language. Most of the Highlanders were Roman Catholic and some of them spoke only Gaelic. Many of the English settlers were merchants and public officials; this group tended to dominate the colony's commercial and political life. The 380 Loyalists who stayed on the Island following the American Revolution became prosperous farmers and merchants who founded several communities, including Bedeque. Although the Irish did not come in large numbers until the 1840s, by the 1820s many Irish lived in Charlottetown.

Regardless of ethnic background, pioneer life was basically the same for everyone. Most work was done manually. Farmers broadcast seeds by hand, harvested the grain with scythes, gathered it with wooden rakes and threshed the grain by beating it upon the ground with flails. They cleaned the grain by tossing it into the air and letting the wind carry off the lighter chaff. The first mechanical threshers, powered by a horse walking on a treadmill, appeared in 1828. As late as 1791, there was only one road on the Island (it joined Covehead and Charlottetown). A trip from the capital to Princetown could take up to two weeks. To solve this problem, the government compelled every male over the age of twenty-one to work eight hours on the roads at least four days each year.

The first settlers had little time to plan their houses, which were usually small log cabins made from newly cut trees. When the land was cleared, they had more time to decide on the type of house they wanted. Of course, the wealthier the family was, the more choices it had. The actual building depended upon the architectural style popular at the time, the building materials available (wood, brick or Island sandstone), the climate and the ethnic background of the owners. Neighbours frequently joined in house-raising frolics to help new families erect their homes before winter. Food and drink were provided, and everyone stayed after supper for singing and dancing to the music of the violin. To keep out the cold, the settlers filled the spaces between the round logs with moss, mud and wood chips. A large fireplace provided warmth, light and heat for cooking. In winter evenings, the pioneers rolled a huge log onto the fire to keep it burning all night. Hot embers, placed in metal containers, served as temporary hand and foot warmers.

The farmers left the stumps of the cleared trees in the ground to rot and planted potatoes around them, leaving fields that appeared to be covered with small mole-hills. The major crops were oats, wheat, barley, flax, peas, turnips and hay. The settlers' diet consisted of oatmeal, porridge, potatoes, pickled herring and cod, supplemented by wild berries, shellfish, ducks and geese in season.

Surplus potatoes and oats were sold in Newfoundland and Nova Scotia, and the money was used to purchase imported tea, tobacco, nails, molasses, rum, sugar and manufactured goods. The settlers made most of their own clothing and furniture. Flannel underwear and linen sheets made from the flax they grew were rough and scratchy.

The division of labour based upon gender was not usually an issue in pioneer times. Men and women did what had to be done. If this meant that females worked in the fields or chased bears away from the gardens, then so it was. Since most work was done in the home, the division of labour between home and the workplace did not arise. The preparation of food and clothing, and the creation of such necessities as soap, medicines and candles, required considerable skill. Even the well-to-do lady was expected to have mastered the domestic arts and to instruct her servants in these. Although there were marriages of love, the large amount of work that needed to be done in each household meant that practical considerations often took priority. Widowed women were highly valued and usually remarried relatively quickly.

Labour was highly valued, and parents were often dependent upon their children's work, especially when cash and hired help were in short supply. In 1820, for example, Walter Johnstone observed the following family situation in his travels through P.E.I.:

In the morning I was awoke with the sound of whistling, so loud as to be heard through the whole house. I rose in haste to see what was become of the older branches of the family, that a boy should be sitting by the fire amusing himself in this way unadmonished by anyone [on a Sunday] ... As I returned in the evening ... I found no little giggling and sport going on among the young people ... [The father] now thought proper to make some apology for the light conduct of his children, which he did in the following manner: "We cannot bring up children here with the sober habits you can in Scotland." "Why?" said I. "Because," replied he, "the children here know that their parents are dependent upon them for help as soon as they are fit to do anything; and if their parents will not give them a good deal of their own way, as other children are getting in the neighbourhood, they will go off and leave them altogether destitute ... If my children that are grown up were to leave me, the old woman and myself ... could not make a living from our farm, after paying wages for working it."

The pioneers had a difficult time. The work of clearing land was brutally hard, and everything around them was new and strange. It was not surprising that they often became very discouraged and homesick. Some even returned home. The range of entertainment was limited. Everyone enjoyed skating, picnics and horseback riding. At "frolics," the entire community pitched in to help build a neighbour's house or barn, or work in the fields in return for food and entertainment. Hunting and fishing provided both enjoyment and fresh meat. Once a week or so the family travelled to the nearest village to sell its produce at the marketplace and buy whatever goods it needed.

For a short period, Charlottetown offered plays in a theatre that seated 200 people. Performances didn't commence until late at night because the actors came to the theatre already dressed and didn't want anyone to see their costumes until the play began. There were several long delays in the show to allow the performers to change costumes, as there were no dressing rooms. The actors changed wherever they could find a room, and the actresses changed across the street at the nearest house.

Religion provided the people with comfort. Church services afforded a familiar atmosphere, and the minister offered spiritual strength. Everyone went to church — except when the snow drifts became too high for the horses to break through. Social gatherings often revolved around the church. The story of Angus Bernard MacEachern describes one of the most prominent religious figures on Prince Edward Island in these early days.

When Father MacEachern arrived on the Island in 1790, he faced a daunting task. Since the deportation of the Acadians in 1758, Roman Catholics in the region had had only one priest in thirty-two years. Angus MacEachern was responsible for the spiritual welfare of Catholics in parts of Nova Scotia, Cape Breton and the Magdalen Islands, as well as on Prince Edward Island. The hardships he endured while travelling from one area to another were almost unbelievable. Without complaint he walked mile after

The Isolation of Pioneer Life

The following account, translated from Gaelic by Sister Margaret MacDonell,
illustrates the feelings of some of the early settlers toward Prince Edward Island:

It is lonely here
in Murray Harbour not knowing English;
it is not what I have been accustomed to,
for I always spoke Gaelic.

My neighbours and I
used to chat at length together;
here I see only scoundrels,
and I do not understand their language.

I am offended at my relatives
who came before me;
they did not tell me about this place
and how it has tried them.
Going through the wilderness
there is nothing but a blazed trail;
this is truly a lonesome place for one who
lives by himself.

A matter of grave concern
as you may surmise,
is the want of footwear and clothing
for each one who needs them.
No one can procure anything
unless he wrests it from the forest.
The length of winter is depressing;
it is fully half one's lifetime.

I'll never send word
to ask friend or relatives to come to this place
with no other resident but myself.
You will not come to live here
if you are in your right mind.

If I knew how to write
so that I could tell my story,
the truth would suffice
to condemn the place;
one need not dissemble.
Though one might do one's best here
when the weather is favourable,
the winter cold is fearsome;
men and beast freeze [to death] ...

mile through the forests, snowshoed over winter trails, rode horse-back through the fields or drove a two-wheeled gig over rough roads. Voyages by sailing vessels in the summer or by ice boat in the winter were taken with little regard for his own personal safety and health.

Since MacEachern's parishioners included Acadians, Highland Scots and Irish, it was fortunate that he spoke French, Gaelic and English. In addition to looking after the religious needs of his people, Bishop MacEachern also cared for their physical well-being. He was largely responsible for the growth in the number of Catholic churches, from the two that existed on the Island when he arrived to fifteen in 1835. The bishop also sought to get the vote for Roman Catholics and helped begin what would become St. Dunstan's College, later part of the University of Prince Edward Island. Bishop MacEachern died in 1835. He is often called the father of Roman Catholicism in Prince Edward Island, and his presence opened a new era in the history of religion on the Island.

Market Day

The market in Charlottetown was the focal point of attraction on Wednesdays and Saturdays. Farmers brought their goods to sell or to exchange for imported essentials. Everywhere there was pandemonium. Customers haggled over prices. Children played games in and around the stalls. Carts, horses and other animals added to the congestion.

The Round Market

The first Charlottetown market was a "frame and picket" building constructed in the centre of Queen Square, where Province House now stands. In 1823 the Round Market pictured here was built. Butter, eggs and poultry were sold from the centre space. Potatoes, oats, hay, fish, wood and carcasses of beef were sold outside.

The Butcher Market

Charlottetown's first permanent market, the Mark Butcher Market House, opened in 1867 on a site approximately where the Confederation Centre theatre stands today. It was 45 metres (148 feet) long by 13.5 metres (44 feet) wide. The upper storey was finished as a public hall. The market burned to the ground in 1902.

The Harris Market

The W. C. Harris Market was designed by William Critchlow Harris in 1904. The second floor was used as a theatre. Fire totally destroyed the building in 1958.

The present Charlottetown market is located on Belvedere Avenue opposite the University of Prince Edward Island.

PEIPARO

SEVEN

William Cooper

PEIPARO

Politics and the
Land Question

According to local legend, one day not too long ago, an old man from Bay Fortune fell asleep in church. When he awoke, the minister was preaching from the Bible about Cain murdering Abel. "You're wrong, sir," said the old man. "It was Pat Pearce who murdered Abell. I can show you the exact spot."

Edward Abell was a fairly well-to-do farmer and merchant who was hired by absentee British landlord James Townshend to look after Lot 56 and to collect rent from the ninety tenants who lived there. Part of his job was to evict tenants who did not pay their rent.

In 1819, Patrick Pearce was a tenant on Lot 56. Pearce owned a beautiful black horse that both Abell and his wife coveted. When Pearce refused to sell the horse, Abell demanded that he pay his rent immediately. Pearce paid his rent, but among the rent money were several Spanish coins that were good on the Island but could not be used in Great Britain. Abell refused to accept these coins, and he demanded British money. If he did not get the proper coins, Abell threatened, he would take Pearce's black horse.

As there were no banks on the Island, Pearce went to his neighbours for help. They traded their Spanish coins for his local coins, and Pearce hurried back to his farm. When he arrived, Edward Abell and his servant were leading his horse away. Thinking that he was just in time to save his horse, Pearce offered the coins to Abell, who refused to accept them and demanded even more money. Pearce was furious, but he set off to borrow the money from his friends.

When Pearce returned, Abell again refused to accept the payment and the two argued angrily. Abell then sat down on a log to watch his servant tether the horse while Pearce went into his house. Pat Pearce took down his gun, fixed a bayonet on it and stabbed Abell twice before the servant could stop him. Abell crawled into the house, and when the servant went for help, Pearce escaped into the woods. Abell died four days later.

The government offered a large reward for Pearce's capture. Although the reward would have paid the average tenant's rent for four years, his neighbours helped him escape. Pearce was never found, and for a long time his house remained vacant, as many people believed it was haunted.

This sensational tale illustrates the land problems that bedevilled Prince Edward Island for over a century and distinguished Island politics from the political situation in the other British North American colonies. Since few landlords resided on P.E.I., they hired local agents to manage their property and collect rent from the tenants. Some absentee landlords never made the effort to collect rent, or waited many years before doing so. Others had difficulty finding competent and conscientious agents on the Island who would not deceive them. In time, some wealthy Islanders acquired large tracts of land, which they rented to the tenants, but these landowners were usually no better than the proprietors who lived off-Island. By the early 1830s, landlords controlled about 90 percent of the colony's farmland, and 65 percent of the Island's 33,000 inhabitants were either tenants or squatters. Six families controlled over one-third of the Island.

The tenants resented putting in years of backbreaking work clearing the land and tilling the soil with no prospect of aquiring their own land. Worse still, since it took many years of work to produce a farm that could generate enough income to pay the landlord, most tenants quickly fell behind in their rent payments. Since non-payment could lead to eviction (without compensation for improvements), this situation naturally created a sense of insecurity and futility among the tenants. Absentee British landlords considered Islanders to be scoundrels, and the tenants thought of the owners, whether Islanders or absentees, as parasites.

During the first thirty years of the 1800s, several unsuccessful attempts were made to solve the land problem. Among other reasons, these attempts failed because the landlords who lived on Prince Edward Island were often able to stop the Island government from doing anything that might harm their interests, and the absentee landlords in Great Britain were wealthy and powerful

Reward
TWENTY POUNDS STERLING

WHEREAS on Tuesday the Twenty-Fourth of August last, a felonious and violent assault was committed upon the Person of the late Edward Abell, Esq. of Bay Fortune, by one PATRICK PEARCE, by mortally wounding him the said Edward Abell, in the body with a fixed bayonet, of which wound the said Edward Abell languished and died on the 28th of the said Month, and whereas the said Murderer has absconded and as yet has eluded the search made for him, by order of the Magistrates of the above names Settlement. A Reward of Twenty Pounds Sterling is hereby offered for the apprehension of the said PATRICK PEARCE, and lodging him in the Gaol of Charlotte-Town, the said Reward to paid on conviction of the Offender. And all his Majesty's Justices of the Peace, Constables, and other Persons are enjoined to use their utmost vigilance in apprehending the said PATRICK PEARCE. And all Masters of Vessels and other Persons leaving this Island are warned to be particularly careful to keep a watchful eye that the said PEARCE is not suffered to make his escape on board of any Boat or Vessel, but should he be discovered in attempting so to do, that he be immediately arrested and placed in the custody of the nearest Magistrate.

The following is a description of the Person of the Offender.

5 feet 6 inches in highth, dark eyes, fair complexion, dark hair, and about 30 years old.

By Order of His Excellency the
Lieut. Governor in Council.

FADE GOFF, D.C.C.

Council Office, Charlotte-Town.

September 7th, 1819.

The Examiner

enough to convince the British government to let them keep their land on the Island. One man who did attempt to help the tenants was William Cooper.

William Cooper

William Cooper was born in England about 1786. After spending many years at sea, he settled on the Island near Bay Fortune, where Edward Abell had been murdered by Pat Pearce. Lord Townshend appointed Cooper to act as his agent. In addition to collecting rent from tenants, Cooper farmed, built ships and erected a mill. Everything went well until Lord Townshend accused Cooper of poor management and fired him.

Cooper switched sides. After working for the landlords, he now became their bitter enemy, and in 1830, he ran for political office. Since he had always sought to help the tenants in his role as an agent, the people of Bay Fortune gave him their support. In 1831, despite a riot on election day that forced Cooper to hide in a barn, he was elected to the Assembly.

Cooper thought that the best way to solve the land question and provide justice for the tenants was to establish a special court, known as an escheat court, which would research which landlords had not paid their quit rents to the government or settled the required number of people on their land. The government would then confiscate the land of those landlords who had not lived up to their agreement, and sell or give it to the tenants. The Escheat movement had originated in 1797, but Cooper gave it momentum.

When the British government rejected the idea of an escheat court, Cooper organized tenants' meetings throughout the Island. He encouraged the tenants not to pay their rents and to create the Escheat Party. Petitions were signed, and rent collectors were threatened by angry groups of tenants armed with pitchforks, stones and other crude weapons. Some rent collectors were hit with frozen cow dung or had the tails of their prize horses cut off. Although some tenants were able to get away with not paying rent, many were arrested or evicted from their land. Cooper, however, paid his own rent and kept his farm, thus enabling his opponents to question his integrity.

The Escheat movement created an Island-wide network of community groups that organized meetings and rallies, drew up petitions and debated political strategy. Thousands of people participated in all sorts of public demonstrations. At one of the largest meetings, 2,000 people attended. Women were as militant as men. Catherine Renahau and her husband, for example, were found guilty of assaulting and wounding a constable sent to collect back rent. In 1839, when a constable came to seize the MacLeods' cattle in payment for their overdue rent, Mrs. MacLeod used a pike to drive him away. Several years earlier, when Constable Donald McVarish had been confronted by an angry group of three men and two women tenants, he had drawn his pistol and pointed it at Isabella MacDonald, who, although well advanced in pregnancy, appeared to the constable to be the most violent member of the group. After McVarish had been stripped of his gun and had promised never to return, Isabella gave him a parting shot with a board.

At a meeting of 700 angry tenants at Hay River in 1836, Cooper's actions so annoyed the governor that he ordered Cooper to apologize to the government. When Cooper refused, the governor prevented him from sitting in the Assembly. The people, however, supported Cooper's ideas. In the next election, the Escheat Party won eighteen of twenty-four seats and gained control of the Assembly. The following year, the Assembly sent Cooper to London to convince the British government of the need for an escheat court. To save money, he travelled third class aboard a lumber ship. He had been given a letter of introduction to the corridors of power by the Island's governor, but unknown to him, the governor had also written another letter to London which criticized Cooper's character. As a result, the British government would not talk with Cooper. For three months he was put off with delays and excuses. He finally returned to the Island in defeat. Great Britain, it seemed, would never accept the idea of an escheat court.

Although Cooper was elected again in 1842, many people had grown tired of promises that brought no results. In 1849, Cooper and his family sailed to California during the gold rush. Cooper did not stay long, but his family remained. His wife, a daughter and a son died of cholera, and the Aboriginal inhabitants killed three of his remaining sons. Although Cooper remained in the Island legislature until 1862, he gradually lost interest in politics and turned to shipbuilding. He died in 1867.

George Coles and Responsible Government

George Coles continued the opposition to the landlords started by Cooper. He was more moderate than his predecessor. Instead of using violence and threats to get his way, Coles believed that Great Britain would accept changes only if they occurred slowly and gradually.

Coles was born on a farm in Charlottetown Royalty in 1810. After helping his father on the farm for many years, he decided to start his own business. He was not well educated, but through hard work he became a successful manufacturer of beer and liquor. He also owned a steam mill, managed a prosperous farm and rented out houses in Charlottetown. By age thirty-five he was fairly wealthy. He was also an excellent speaker who could quickly spot the weaknesses in his opponents' arguments.

In 1842, George Coles was elected to the Assembly. He believed that the first step towards solving the land problem was to change the format of the Island government, which at this time was still largely controlled by the governor, who was appointed by the government of Great Britain. The governor listened to the advice of the Council (which he appointed) and to the Assembly (which was elected), but he did not have to accept their advice. Because the governor had to sign each bill before it became law, he was the most important man on the Island. The Council was next in political importance and was dominated by a small group of related families (such as the Wrights, the Havilands and the Palmers) who controlled much of the Island's wealth. All bills passed by the Assembly needed the Council's approval before being sent on to the governor.

The governor and the Council were often sympathetic to the landlords or were landlords themselves. Coles, therefore, believed that the only way the tenants could get a fair deal was to make the Assembly more powerful. He began to push for responsible government, which meant that to remain in office, the Council had to have the support of the Assembly, and that the Council's members would be chosen from the Assembly, much as the Cabinet today is responsible to the elected representatives in the provincial legislature. In addition, the governor would be required to sign all bills passed by the Council that concerned purely local matters. If responsible government was granted, the Assembly would have most of the power.

The idea of responsible government was not new. Reformers in Nova Scotia, New Brunswick and the other British North American colonies were also struggling to achieve it. Nova Scotia was granted responsible government in 1848. Great Britain, however, thought that the people of Prince Edward Island were too poor and uneducated to make it work. Finally, in 1851, the Island was given responsible government, and George Coles became the first premier. The governor, however, retained the power to protect the landlords' property rights and to safeguard the interests of the mother country.

More Attempts at Land Reform

The new government's first attempts to help the tenants failed. Great Britain rejected a proposal to increase the tax on all uncultivated land, which the Assembly had hoped would encourage the landlords to sell their land. Great Britain also rejected a bill that would have forced landlords to reimburse evicted tenants for improvements they had made to the land. The Land Purchase Act of 1853 was more successful. This bill allowed the Island government to buy any estate exceeding 400 hectares (1,000 acres), if the landlord was willing to sell. The land was then to be sold to the tenants by the government. In the next seven years the Worrell and Selkirk estates were purchased and resold under the provisions of this act.

Progress was being made, but change came slowly. Many landlords refused to sell their estates, and the Island government had little money with which to buy their land. Many tenants hoped that Great Britain would lend money to the Island or force the landlords to sell their land for a fair price. When the British government rejected this solution, the tenants took matters into their own hands.

In 1864, a Tenant League was formed. Each member pledged not to pay rent and to support other tenants who refused to honour their leases. By depriving the landlords of this revenue, the league hoped to force the proprietors to sell their land at reasonable rates. Politicians were excluded from the league as they were perceived to have failed the tenants. In less than a year, membership swelled to about eleven thousand.

On March 17, 1865, the Tenant League organized a march through Charlottetown. About five hundred demonstrators crossed the ice on sleighs and horseback from Southport and marched through the city to the accompaniment of a musical band. During this otherwise peaceful demonstration, Deputy Sheriff James Curtis attempted to arrest Sam Fletcher for non-payment of his rent, for which he was two years in arrears. Fletcher knocked the sheriff to the ground and escaped.

Thus challenged, the government ordered the sheriff to organize a posse to arrest Fletcher. The posse that assembled on April 7 was a motley group of about one hundred and fifty conscripts who proceeded on horse, foot and in wagons. Some members of the group sang a pro-tenant rights song as they marched along. The expedition took no one by surprise. As the posse marched the eighteen miles to Fletcher's farm, the tenants along the way blew their trumpets to warn Fletcher of its advance. These long horns were normally used to inform workers in the fields that it was dinner-time. During the days of the Tenant League, however, they served to warn the community of the approach of the rent collector.

It was springtime and the clay roads had been reduced to swamps of mud, slush and water. This, plus the political divisions within the posse, did not help the men's spirits. It was Sam Fletcher's tactics, however, that created the most consternation and exposed the posse to public ridicule. No two stories of the events are identical, but all agree that Fletcher outsmarted the sheriff and his men. At a blacksmith's shop near Vernon River, a crude fort staffed with cannons delayed the posse until closer inspection revealed that the fort was constructed of old stove pipes, and those who held the guns were only straw scarecrows with paper faces and nightcaps. Later, as the posse approached Fletcher's property, the men were amazed to see Sam calmly leaning against his gatepost, apparently waiting for them. After carefully surrounding him, the men were embarrassed once again. The clothes were Sam's, but the body was straw. Dispirited, the posse returned to Charlottetown without Sam Fletcher.

Edward Whelan, the editor of the *Examiner*, wrote scathingly, "Up to Friday last, Sam Fletcher was an insignificant individual. He is now the hero of the hour; and the ease with which he had turned his back upon the concentrated force of the county ... thereby covered it with ridicule." Fletcher had become a popular symbol of successful resistance to authority. The Island government finally sent for the British troops in Halifax to keep control. The disobedience stopped, but the problems remained. Sam Fletcher was never apprehended. Although rumours persisted that Fletcher changed his name and remained on Prince Edward Island, he apparently died off-Island.

Persuaded by these disturbances, some landlords decided to sell their holdings. The large Cunard estate, for example, was sold in 1866. Five years later, only one-quarter of the Island remained in the large proprietors' hands. When P.E.I. entered Confederation in 1873, the federal government promised the Island $800,000 to help solve the land problems. Two years later, the provincial government passed the compulsory Land Purchase Act to facilitate additional land sales. By 1895, the government had bought all the estates, and most of the tenants had become property owners.

EIGHT

The Empress on the Montague River

The Golden Age

The period from 1830 to 1880 is sometimes called the "golden age" of Prince Edward Island. The Island prospered during this time. There were still poor people, but Islanders were generally doing very well.

Farming

The economy of Prince Edward Island in the nineteenth century was based on the small family farm. If the farmer prospered, so too did the merchants and manufacturers. Island crops were so plentiful that oats were exported to Great Britain; cattle, sheep and potatoes went to Newfoundland; potatoes were shipped to Bermuda; and grain, pork and potatoes were sold in Nova Scotia and New Brunswick.

Much of the credit for the growth in agriculture belonged to the many agricultural societies organized between 1825 and 1850, which encouraged farmers to use modern farming methods. They organized fairs, offered prizes, gave talks, and imported new grains and farming machines. Clydesdale horses; Ayrshire, Shorthorn, Hereford and Angus beef cattle; Leicester sheep; and Yorkshire, Berkshire and Tomworth pigs were imported to improve Island livestock. Farmers began rotating their crops rather than planting the same grain year after year and ruining the soil. Fertilizer was particularly important; without it, the Island soil soon became exhausted. Fish, lobster shells, barnyard manure and mussel mud were the most widely used fertilizers during this period.

Mussel Mud

The term *mussel mud* is not quite correct. Although there were mussel shells in the mud close to the shore, it was the large amount of oyster shells that provided valuable lime for the soil. These shell beds were usually about 2 metres (6.5 feet) deep, although in the St. Peter's Bay area, they were up to 10 metres (33 feet) deep. Despite its advantages, mussel mud was not used very much until the 1860s because it was too difficult to shovel out of the water.

The invention of a horse-powered machine to dig the mud in winter alleviated this problem. Dressed in warm layers of winter wool, farmers gathered with their sleds near the great wooden mud diggers to get a load. In such popular sites as North River, South West River, Brudenell and St. Peter's Bay, as many as a hundred farmers would huddle together in the cold, waiting to get their sleighload of fertilizer.

In 1916, the government began digging in St. Peter's Bay. The mussel mud was loaded onto railway flatcars and delivered inland to areas that otherwise could not get fertilizer. This "mud special" continued running into the 1920s, but as artificial fertilizers became more available, mussel mud and mud diggers declined in popularity.

Merchants and Mills

Agricultural growth also benefited urban areas. Merchants provided the farmers with goods to meet their needs. In the second half of the nineteenth century, all types of mills sprang up. In 1871, there were more than five hundred carding, grist, saw, fulling, dressing and shingle mills. In addition to the mills, small factories were erected to manufacture or process goods such as leather, wheels, furniture, shoes, horse-drawn buggies, tobacco, beer, fish oil, bricks, sleighs, clothes, pianos, hay elevators, mowing machines, iron plows and potato hillers. With manufacturing, as with agriculture, the Island was generally self-sufficient. It was during this period that prominent Island business people such as R. T. Holman, M. F. Schurman, Malcolm McLeod, J. C. Pope, David Rogers, John L. Mackinnon and John Linkletter got their start.

The story of Robert T. Holman is fairly typical of the rise of the merchant class on the Island at this time. When his father died in 1846, thirteen-year-old Robert Holman left school to take a job in a store in Saint John, New Brunswick. During the next eleven years, he moved from town to town. In 1848, he was a clerk in a Boston drugstore. Two years later he arrived in Charlottetown to work for one of his brothers. From Charlottetown he moved to St. Eleanors and then to Summerside. In each location, Robert was hired by a member of his family. Finally, in 1856, he opened a small store of his own on Water Street in Summerside, where he put his experience and ideas into practice.

Robert had a genius for commerce. His store was always orderly and neat, and he looked after the smallest details. He was also honest. When Robert made a promise, he would rather lose money than break his word. Customers who were unhappy with their goods could either exchange them or get their money back, a benefit few other stores offered.

Holman kept in close touch with the farmers, which helped him decide which goods to buy for his store. Good fortune also helped the growth of his business: a relative in California left him a large amount of money, as did his brother James. In 1857, Holman had only one small store. By 1893, he had a three-storey brick building, a large freight house, a warehouse and sixty employees. Not

Inventors and Inventions

As the following list of patents granted between 1837 and 1873 indicates, necessity was the mother of invention in the farming sector.

Date	Patent Holder	Location	Invention
1837:	Stephen Bovyer	Charlottetown	A device for horse-powered threshing machines
1860:	John Burns	Pownal	Wooden carriage springs
1860:	George Jenkins	Lot 49	Machine for digging potatoes
1860:	William MacKenzie	Lot 48	Machine for digging potatoes
1868:	George Millner	Charlottetown	Machine for sowing grain
1869:	Rev. James Burns	Pownal	Wooden carriage springs
1870:	William Biggs	Tryon	Centre vent water wheel
1871:	Watson Duchemin	Charlottetown	Egg carriers
1871:	George Millner	Charlottetown	Milk pail
1872:	William MacKenzie	Lot 48	Mussel-mud fork
1872:	George Millner	Charlottetown	Potato digger
1872:	Neil Taylor	Lot 61	Stumping machine
1872:	Abraham Gill	Lot 34	Hay carrier
1873:	Robert Longworth Fox	Charlottetown	Heating equipment

satisfied with owning the largest department store on the Island, Holman expanded his interests. He built a meat and poultry cannery, began a lobster factory and became a shipbuilder and owner. When R. T. Holman died in 1906, he had created one of the best family-run businesses in the Maritimes.

Fishing

Just as agriculture and commerce flourished by the mid-nineteenth century, so did the fishery. Islanders caught enough fish to satisfy the domestic market, and sold dried cod, salt herring, mackerel, gaspereaux and fish oil to the United States. By 1890, Island fishers realized that profits could also be made from lobster and oyster fishing, and these two seafoods soon dominated Island fisheries.

At mid-century there was no economical method of keeping lobsters alive until they reached the market. Unlike cod or mackerel, lobsters could not be dried, salted or pickled. The advent of lobster-canning procedures changed this crustacean from a fertilizer into a delicacy. Between 1873 and 1883, the number of canneries on the Island rose dramatically from two to about one hundred, and the value of the fishery increased from $218,000 to $2,000,000.

When lobster catches began to decline, the federal government established two separate lobster-fishing seasons in 1889 and made it illegal to keep lobsters with the eggs attached. Later, minimum sizes were established and lobster fishers were licenced. International treaties had always banned Americans from taking lobsters and shellfish from Island waters, and lobster catches remained high. In the twentieth century, better traps and such technological changes as gasoline-powered engines, refrigeration and faster transportation led to more efficient marketing and processing.

Shipbuilding

One of the main reasons for the prosperity on the Island in the mid-nineteenth century was the growth of shipbuilding. Islanders lived by producing and exporting fish, timber and agricultural produce. They required ships to transport these goods and to import manufactured products and other items not found at home. The Island was perfectly suited for shipbuilding. All that was needed to set up a shipyard was a sheltered harbour with a deep body of water at high tide and a good supply of timber. By the 1830s, shipbuilding yards were scattered over a hundred different locations, and Islanders made more money sailing and selling ships than they did exporting their agricultural goods.

Shipbuilders such as Lemuel Cambridge, William Ellis, James Peake, James Yeo, John Douse, James Duncan, William Richards, L. C. Owen, J. C. Pope and William Heard gained reputations for their well-built vessels. As a rule, Maritimers did not build fast clipper ships but concentrated on building vessels designed to carry large quantities of goods. Many ship owners were also shipbuilders whose main goal was to sell their ships in Great Britain. Not every type of sailing ship was built in each port. Shipyards in Mount Stewart concentrated on brigantines; those in Grand River and Port Hill preferred barques and barquentines; and those in Souris and New Glasgow built schooners. In general, vessels made in Prince Edward Island were smaller than those constructed in either Nova Scotia or New Brunswick.

The timber to build ships or to export was usually cut in winter and hauled out of the woods by teams of horses or oxen. Some farmers earned extra money in the winters this way. Often, however, landlords had their tenants strip the timber from their land or forced the tenants to do the work to pay their debts. Shipbuilding began with the approach of spring, and the Island shipyards came alive with the sound of axes thudding into wood.

The vessels' keels and frames were made mainly from hardwood trees; juniper and spruce were used for planking the frames and the decks; pine made the best masts and spars. Saws ripped timber into planks, and the planks for the hulls were then placed in steam boxes to soften. Shipwrights, carpenters, sail makers, chandlers, blacksmiths, riggers and spar makers were needed for the construction of a sound vessel. Shipbuilding encouraged the growth of these occupations, which in turn brought prosperity to the nearby villages. Summerside, for example, owed its growth to shipbuilding. By 1871, Summerside had become second in size only to Charlottetown.

Everyone looked forward to the day a new ship was launched. Schools and stores closed, and students and workers took the day off. Ladies and gentlemen dressed in their finest clothes, and the vessel itself was often gaily decorated with flags. When the shipbuilders began to grease the slip, the crowd became silent. A tense moment was at hand: would she float? Before the blocks holding back the vessel were knocked out, a bottle of champagne was broken over the hull and the vessel was christened. When the stern hit the water and the boat floated, a great cheer burst from the crowd.

After the launching, many vessels were filled with squared timber and sailed to Great Britain. There, both the timber and the ship were sold. Other vessels were sold in Nova Scotia and New Brunswick. Newfoundland sailors bought schooners and brigantines for sealing and fishing. Some Island shipbuilders kept their vessels and used them to carry potatoes, oats, wheat, lumber, fish and livestock to Newfoundland, Nova Scotia, the United States and the West Indies. Between 1830 and 1873, Island builders launched more than three thousand new ships.

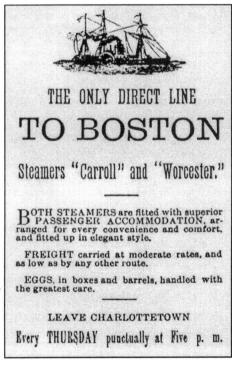

THE ONLY DIRECT LINE

TO BOSTON

Steamers "Carroll" and "Worcester."

BOTH STEAMERS are fitted with superior PASSENGER ACCOMMODATION, arranged for every convenience and comfort, and fitted up in elegant style.

FREIGHT carried at moderate rates, and as low as by any other route.

EGGS, in boxes and barrels, handled with the greatest care.

LEAVE CHARLOTTETOWN

Every THURSDAY punctually at Five p. m.

The Island Magazine

Summerside Pioneer, May 1881

James Yeo was one of the Island's most successful shipbuilders. He was born with two disadvantages. He had a poker spine, which meant that to bend over, he had to flex at the hips. Despite this problem, Yeo was strong and had great physical endurance. His second disadvantage was to be born into a poor British family. However, when James Yeo died, at age seventy-nine, he was the richest man on Prince Edward Island.

The first thirty years of Yeo's life were filled with unhappiness. His wife, who gave birth to three sons, died in 1818, and Yeo began to drink heavily. Partly as a result of this, his small business failed. The next year, his luck changed. James was hired by British businessman Thomas Burnard to manage his lumber gangs and to help with Burnard's store and shipbuilding business on P.E.I.

In the next two decades, Yeo combined hard work, intelligence and ruthlessness to make a fortune. When Thomas Burnard died in England, Yeo apparently pretended he was Burnard's agent and collected money from those who were in debt to Burnard. James Yeo used this money to go into business for himself. He became a lumber dealer and a storekeeper in Port Hill, and master of a small schooner. He later pretended to own much of the land in Prince County and, it was said, sent in his own men to cut valuable timber. Because many of the tenants were illiterate and could not read their leases, Yeo was able to get away with this deceit.

The hardworking Yeo rode all over Prince County to supervise his operations. Sometimes his horse trotted on through the night as he slept in the saddle. Yeo had an excellent memory and could quickly calculate crop figures and business statistics in his head. As he became more powerful, he was elected to the government and was made a justice of the peace.

Yeo's entire family helped with his businesses. His second wife and their five daughters managed his store at Port Hill, which sold the tobacco, salt, tea, rum, nails, shoes, molasses, meat, cloth, rope and saws that Yeo's ships imported from Great Britain and Nova Scotia. His sons helped buy lumber, oats, livestock and salted cod, which were exported to Great Britain in Yeo's ships. His two youngest sons and his sons-in-law built more than two hundred vessels. Many of these sailed unfinished to England, where they were completed at the family's shipyard, which was managed by Yeo's oldest son, William. With his family's aid, James Yeo became the largest shipbuilder on the Island.

During his life, Yeo was responsible for the construction of about 350 vessels, 250 of which he sold in Great Britain. The others were used to carry agricultural and lumber goods to Britain, and to return with immigrants and manufactured items not available on the Island. Although he was not a popular man, by the time James Yeo died of pneumonia in 1868, he had done much to develop the Island's economy.

Urban Life

In 1821, Charlottetown consisted of approximately three hundred white or straw-coloured wooden buildings and had a population of about two thousand. As in London and Edinburgh, the streets were laid out in a grid pattern, with a main central area (Queen Square) reserved for such important public buildings as the court house. Smaller open green spaces were situated in each quadrant of the grid. Beyond the 500 town lots lay a belt of farmland (the Royalty) for urban dwellers to grow their own food. The wide, dimly lit streets often turned into mud holes in spring and fall, and into dust bowls in the summer. Outdoor privies, horse stables, vagabond cows and pigs, and open cesspools all added their unique aromas to city life.

In many rural areas the settlers had precarious links to the outside world. When overseas mail arrived, it was stored in Charlottetown until someone came to collect it. Sometimes the local newspaper alerted its rural readership by publishing a list of the unclaimed letters. Beginning in 1827, postal carriers delivered the mail once a week to local post offices. The isolation, the hard work and the lack of entertainment perhaps explain the one gallon of rum that was imported for every man, woman and child in 1830.

NINE

Province House, Charlottetown

Confederation

In 1860, British North America was a collection of sparsely populated colonies that knew very little about each other. In fact, only two of the Fathers of Confederation who came to Prince Edward Island in 1864 had previously been to the Maritimes. Upper Canadians provided the initiative for Confederation. In 1841, Great Britain had united Upper Canada (Ontario) and Lower Canada (Quebec) into the Province of Canada. By the 1860s, however, this union had become unworkable. Many of the Protestant, English-speaking inhabitants of Upper Canada disliked and distrusted the Roman Catholic French Canadians in the eastern half of the province, and this feeling was mutual. Unable to achieve a stable majority, the government floundered in indecision, and the economy stagnated. To the south, the United States was engaged in a bloody civil war, and some American politicians were talking about marching north into Canada at war's end.

The Charlottetown Conference

Some people believed that a union of all the British North American colonies might solve these and other problems. Unity would provide better military defence. A federal union would divide Upper and Lower Canada into separate provinces, each with control over matters of religion and language. A larger country would help the economy. Tariff barriers between provinces would be removed, and interprovincial trade would benefit. In 1864, prominent Canadian politicians John A. Macdonald, George Brown, Alexander Galt and George-Étienne Cartier joined forces to work toward a federation of all British North America. Their most difficult task would be to convince the Atlantic colonies to enter the union.

The Maritime colonies had briefly discussed the idea of a Maritime Union. This merger, some Maritime politicians believed, would turn three relatively weak colonies into a single, more powerful body. The new colony would save money and eliminate such problems as coping with three different currencies and sets of laws. Maritime Union, however, had few supporters. Each colony was jealous of its own rights, and contact among the three provinces was sporadic. Winter travel was particularly difficult. One Islander complained about the possibility of sending representatives to government meetings on the mainland: would they be "expected to take pole in hand and leap from iceberg to iceberg across the Straits in the dead of winter?"

Although Prince Edward Island was unenthusiastic about Maritime Union, the government agreed to attend a conference on the topic — but only if the meeting was held on the Island. When the Canadian government learned about this conference, it asked permission to attend and present an alternative proposal. Only then was a place and date set for the meeting — in Charlottetown on September 1, 1864. The course of Canadian history was about to be dramatically changed.

Islanders displayed a general lack of interest in the conference. When the delegates from Nova Scotia and New Brunswick arrived in Charlottetown on August 31, there was no one to meet them. Everyone, it seemed, was at the circus, which was making its first appearance on the Island in twenty-one years. When the Canadians arrived the next day aboard the steamboat *Queen Victoria*, they also received an unenthusiastic welcome. Only provincial secretary W. H. Pope was present to greet them. A fisher rowed him out to the *Queen Victoria* in an old oyster boat with two jars of molasses in the stern and a barrel of flour in the bow. Unperturbed, the Canadians, according to George Brown, "dressed [themselves] like Mr. Christopher Columbus."

The delegates met in Province House. The Maritime delegation agreed to postpone discussion of Maritime Union until it had heard the Canadian proposal. Vigorous and reasoned speeches from John A. Macdonald, George-Étienne Cartier, Alexander Galt, D'Arcy

McGee and George Brown convinced the Maritime representatives that Confederation might be a good idea, and they agreed to meet again later in the fall in Quebec City.

The six days of meetings in Charlottetown were accompanied by endless parties. The Canadians had brought along $13,000 worth of champagne to facilitate the discussions, and the Islanders wined and dined the delegates in style. The crowning event was a grand ball at Province House. The library became the refreshment room, and the assembly chamber served as the dance floor. From ten at night until one in the morning the delegates and their wives danced to the sounds of two bands. Then dinner was served — beef, ham, salmon, lobsters, oysters, fruits, pastries and wine — followed by three hours of speeches. The delegates toasted each other and sang "For They Are Jolly Good Fellows." Cartier concluded the banquet by singing "God Save the Queen" in English and French. The next day the delegates left for a tour of the Maritimes before proceeding to Quebec City to hammer out a new constitution.

Charcoal study of *The Fathers of Confederation*, by Robert Harris

National Gallery of Canada

The Quebec Conference

Thirty-three delegates, including two members from Newfoundland, attended the conference in Quebec City in October. The seven delegates from Prince Edward Island were politicians George Coles, John H. Gray, T. H. Haviland, A. D. MacDonald, Edward Palmer, W. H. Pope and Edward Whelan.

It rained the entire seventeen days. One reporter wrote, "What can I tell you? Almost nothing. It is raining. It rains every day, making the stay in Quebec — normally so gay and amusing when the weather is fine — disagreeable in the extreme."

The delegates met every day but Sunday, from eleven in the morning until four in the afternoon. Smaller, informal meetings took place at any time. After the first week, the delegates also met in the evening from 7:30 P.M. to midnight. The festive mood of Charlottetown had dissipated, and arguments raged back and forth. This was where John A. Macdonald was at his best. When discussions became heated, he was usually able to cool down tempers. He wined and dined the delegates and their wives and children. Edward Whelan of the Charlottetown *Examiner* noted, "The Canadians are the most tireless dancers I have ever seen. They do not seem to miss a dance during the live-long night. They are cunning fellows; and there's no doubt that it is all done for a political purpose. They know that if they can dance themselves into the affections of the wives and daughters of the Maritimers, the men will certainly become an easy target."

Constitution making, however, was serious business, and the P.E.I. delegates were vigilant in protecting provincial interests. It soon became evident that the Canadians did not envision the Island as having much to say regarding national matters. Instead of provincial equality in the Senate, there was to be regional equality. The Atlantic provinces, Ontario and Quebec were each to receive the same number of senators. In the House of Commons, Islanders sought six seats, but the Canadian delegates insisted on the principle of representation by population, and Prince Edward Island was allotted only five members for its population of about eighty thousand.

The delegates from P.E.I. soon gained a reputation as obstructionists. They not only complained about representation, but also about the financial arrangements. When they requested a grant of $800,000 to buy the properties of the landlords, the other delegates rejected the idea. At the conclusion of the Quebec Conference, the Island delegation was divided — Gray, Haviland, Pope and Whelan favoured Confederation, whereas Coles, MacDonald and Palmer opposed it. Most Islanders, however, turned against union, and the Island government vetoed Confederation by a combined vote of thirty-six to five in 1865, and thirty-four to seven the following year.

Opposition to Confederation

Prince Edward Island rejected Confederation for several reasons. Many Islanders favoured a federal union if advantageous terms could be arranged; however, Prince Edward Island's political and economic needs had been largely ignored by the constitution makers. After many years of struggle, the Island was finally prospering, so there was no urgent need to change its political situation. Shipbuilding and lumbering brought in needed revenue. The 1854 reciprocity — or free trade — agreement with the United States had opened new markets for Island farm produce. As a result of this progress, the population had increased from 47,000 in 1841 to 81,000 in 1861. New communities were emerging in every part of the Island, and roads linked one end of the province to the other.

A growing pride and sense of identity accompanied this economic surge. Although race, religion, politics and class differences divided Islanders, the Northumberland Strait provided a sense of uniqueness. According to Island historian David Weale, Island identity was closely related to the rural nature of the colony. "The habits, morals, way of thinking, temperament, dialect, dress, cuisine, pastimes, in short, the entire culture and ethos of the Island, were thoroughly farm-orientated .... The Islanders, then, shared not only an agricultural vocation, but also a distinct system of values and ideals which grew out of this way of life. The Colony ... idealized such qualities as simplicity and frugality; and the residents tended to be extremely suspicious of trends and events in the outside world — particularly in the big cities — which threatened to undermine these basic virtues."

Entry into Confederation would end the province's autonomy and jeopardize its newly won responsible government, for nothing more than becoming an insignificant partner in a larger political unit. The Island, declared one native, would be "like a poor maiden married to a rich gentleman, who priding himself on the superiority of his birth and riches, would not scruple to treat her as a menial servant rather than as a beloved spouse." How could five representatives in distant Ottawa protect the interests of Prince Edward Islanders?

The next attempt to change Islanders' minds came from Canada in 1869. A year earlier, Benjamin Butler, a member of the government of the United States, had visited Prince Edward Island to discuss a trade agreement between the United States and the Island. Canadian Prime Minister John A. Macdonald feared that the Americans planned to use Prince Edward Island as a military base to attack the mainland. The colony was also in a strategic position to control the fisheries and smuggle goods into Canada. Macdonald acted quickly. He sent delegates to the colony to talk with the Island government. In December 1869, Canada offered the Island more money and promised to solve the absentee landlord problem. Once again, the colony rejected Confederation.

Confederation Timeline

Charlottetown Conference:	September 1864
Quebec Conference:	October 1864
London Conference:	1866
Confederation:	July 1, 1867
Manitoba enters:	1870
British Columbia enters:	1871
Prince Edward Island enters:	1873
Alberta and Saskatchewan become provinces:	1905
Newfoundland enters:	1949

Prince Edward Island Enters Confederation

In 1871, the Island government decided to build a railway spanning the 147 miles from Alberton to Georgetown. Branch lines to Souris and Tignish followed later. It would be the first railway on the Island, and the idea proved very popular. Everyone would prosper — or so many people believed. Construction workers would be needed, factories would be built and farmers would be able to transport their crops to the towns more rapidly.

The railway branch lines crisscrossed the Island. Every village wanted to be connected to the main line. The terms of the construction contract established a fixed price per mile but set no limit on the number of miles to be constructed, and thus the railroad wound around the countryside. One-third of the line consisted of curves. The company built an average of one train station for every three miles of track. As a result, the railway cost far more than expected, and the provincial debt increased from $250,000 to more than $4 million. The lenders wanted their money back, but neither Great Britain nor Island banks would lend the government more money unless P.E.I. agreed to join Confederation, becoming part of a larger financial union with greater credit worthiness.

Final Terms of Confederation for P.E.I.

Canada to assume the Island's debts and liabilities, and to operate and maintain the railway.

Debt allowance raised to $50 per person.

Canada to maintain "efficient and continuous" telegraphic and steamship communication with the mainland.

Provincial government to receive $52,000 annually plus $0.80 per person.

Prince Edward Island to receive six Members of Parliament. (The population had increased since 1864.)

The Island to receive $800,000 to buy land from the proprietors.

At this crucial time, Prime Minister John A. Macdonald presented the Island with another offer. The Island's huge debt, plus promises to help solve the land problems, finally persuaded P.E.I. to enter Confederation on July 1, 1873; however, as the following statement from *The Patriot* indicates, Confederation was not popular. "At 12 o'clock noon, the Dominion Flag was run up the flag staffs at Government House and the Colonial Building, and a salute of 21 guns was fired from St. George's battery and from H.M.S.

Spartan now in port. The church and city bells rang out a lively peel ... But among the people who thronged the streets there was no enthusiasm ... After the reading of the Proclamation was concluded, the gentlemen on the balcony gave a cheer, but the three persons below ... responded never a word."

TEN

Acadian Home in Rustico, by Robert Harris

Hard Times after Confederation

The late nineteenth and early twentieth centuries brought hard economic times for many Islanders. The advent of steel and steam effectively ended the prosperous shipbuilding industry. Even if wood, wind and sails had been able to compete against steel and steam, the Island's shipbuilding industry would have foundered because the supply of trees suitable for large masts had been depleted, and lumber had to be imported from New Brunswick, which increased the price of the ships. By 1880, the "golden age" of shipbuilding had ended.

Poor forest management had decimated the Island's timber reserves, and destructive land-use practices reduced farming incomes. Ottawa's adoption of the protective tariff in 1879 aided industrial growth, but raised the prices of manufactured goods and did little to help agriculture and fishing. The federal government's decision in the twentieth century to increase freight rates on the Intercolonial Railway that linked the Maritimes with central Canadian markets further damaged the economy.

In despair of ever finding employment on the Island, many Islanders left for the United States, especially the New England states. The population, which had gradually increased from 88,000 at Confederation to 109,000 in 1881, steadily declined. Between 1870 and 1900, approximately 30,000 Islanders left the province. The population bottomed out at 86,000 in 1924. As the Island's population diminished and immigrants flowed into the Canadian West, P.E.I.'s percentage of Canada's total population fell from 2.5 in 1881 to 1.0 in 1921, and to 0.8 in 1941. Many Islanders went to Boston, which had commercial ties with the Island. In fact, some wealthy Islanders preferred to shop in Boston rather than in Montreal or Toronto, and Maritime women trained in nursing schools in New England rather than in central Canada. Although emigration to the "Boston States" and elsewhere relieved the province of its surplus labour, it tended to be the young, educated people who left the Island. This constant drain of skilled people no doubt had a detrimental effect on subsequent economic development. It certainly resulted in a high percentage of the population being over seventy years of age and placed an increased tax burden on the employed people who remained behind. In 1931, for example, the average age of an Island citizen was thirty: the highest in Canada. With no large industries, or forest and mineral wealth to tax, P.E.I. began to rely heavily on federal subsidies.

Fox Farming

There was one bright spot on the otherwise rather dismal economic horizon at this time. The development of fox farming at the turn of the century bolstered Islanders' confidence and brought much-needed money to the province. Charles Dalton and Robert Oulton were two fox-farming pioneers on Prince Edward Island.

In the early 1800s, Charles Dalton was an active young man who loved the outdoors. Much of his time, however, was spent working in his father's store at Tignish. To make extra money, Dalton often went fox hunting with his older friend Robert Oulton — live red foxes were needed by American hunting clubs for the fox-and-hound chase. The pelt of the rarer black fox was much more valuable. The guard hairs of the black fox are tipped with silver, hence the term "silver fox." These beautiful pelts were in great demand by the fashion industry. Each man realized that a fortune could be made if black foxes were bred in the same way as farmers breed cows and horses. After several years of working unsuccessfully on their own, Dalton and Oulton decided to work together. They soon discovered that the foxes would not breed unless the fox ranches resembled the animals' natural environment.

The two men established a ranch on Cherry Island near Alberton. To make fox kennels, they nailed a board over one end of a hollow log and filled the log with soft, dry seaweed. To prevent the captive foxes from using their sharp teeth and claws to escape into the woods, the men built fences using special wire netting made in Montreal. Part of each fence was buried deep in the soil so that the

The much-prized silver fox

foxes couldn't escape by digging under the fence. Male and female foxes were kept separate, except at breeding time. Dalton and Oulton also had to learn the animals' diet and habits. They discovered, for example, that a mother fox would kill her young if she was disturbed during whelping season.

In 1896, their fox-breeding program was finally successful. The fortunes of Dalton and Oulton were now secured. In 1900, for instance, a single pelt was sold in London, England, for $1800. The partners wanted to keep their success a secret, and did not even tell their wives and children about the details of the breeding. They discouraged visitors to the ranch and hired a guard to protect the grounds at night. So that no one would discover how valuable the business was, Dalton secretly mailed the pelts from a distant post office or sent them out at night by ship.

Secrets, however, are hard to keep on a small island, and it wasn't long before other people in western Prince County became interested in fox ranching and the wealth it brought. In 1898, Silas and B. I. Rayner, Robert Tuplin and James Gordon formed a partnership with Oulton and Dalton. The Big Six, as they were called, agreed to keep their fox-breeding practices secret and not to produce too many pelts: if a large number of furs were sold, the price of each pelt would decrease. This monopoly of the silver fox industry was broken when Robert Tuplin sold four fox pups to

Robert Holman of Summerside for $10,000 in 1899. The fox boom had begun. Three years later there were approximately three hundred fox ranches on the Island and the industry was valued at $20 million. Fox farming remained profitable until the 1940s. New methods of dyeing, changing fashions, overproduction and the popularity of mink and muskrat furs reduced the demand for silver fox pelts. By 1968, there were only ten fox ranches on the Island. An increase in the price of fox pelts to $600 each in 1976 - 1977 resulted in a renewed interest in fur farming. Since then, prices have fluctuated.

A few reminders of this era in Island life are the distinctive houses that were built with "fox money." Islanders who had lived in shanties and old homesteads moved into grand houses when fox farming made them wealthy. Many of these homes were erected by Will Maynard, an architect and builder. The large "fox houses" had balconies, magnificent woodwork and central heating. Although many of the fox houses that were built between 1913 and 1925 are now deserted or broken-down, some of them have been well kept. They remind us of the brief time when Prince Edward Island was the centre of the world's attention.

The Impact of War

The Boer War (1899 - 1902) temporarily distracted Islanders from their economic woes. Motivated by loyalty to the mother country, thousands of Canadians volunteered to help Great Britain crush the Boers in South Africa and Islanders surpassed all other provinces in their enthusiasm to enlist. "There is something stirring and exciting and tingling about it all even here in this quiet little Island thousands of miles from the seat of war," Lucy Maud Montgomery confided to her diary. "Everyone is intensely interested in the news."

Nurses as well as soldiers travelled to South Africa. The four Island nurses who accompanied the first contingent of soldiers from the Island were led by Georgina Fane Pope, a thirty-seven-year-old native of Charlottetown who had graduated from nursing school in New England. In South Africa, Pope headed the Canadian Army

Nursing Service and was the first Canadian to be awarded the Royal Red Cross. Of the 125 Islanders who served in South Africa, two didn't return.

Island nurses saw active duty in the First World War as well. In addition to Georgina Pope, several other Island women served as nursing sisters in Europe. Souris native Rena Maude McLean, for example, saw duty in France and Greece before her hospital ship was torpedoed and sunk on its return to Halifax in 1918. The following year, the Rena McLean Memorial Hospital opened in Charlottetown to care for convalescent veterans.

On the home front, women in every community organized to provide food, clothes and other necessities for the soldiers overseas. Church groups, the Imperial Order of the Daughters of the Empire, the Women's Institutes, the Women's Patriotic Association and the Red Cross Society all launched fund-raising activities. They provided relief for prisoners of war, knitted socks, made pajamas and underwear, rolled bandages and helped recruit men for the armed forces. Obliged to tend to the family farm or business alone, many women had to cope with mounting inflation and fuel and food rations, while nervously following the news from the front with its

Many were involved in the war effort

seemingly endless lists of dead soldiers. The impact of the war was inescapable. Skating rinks became shooting ranges, and theatres offered military documentaries to boost home morale.

Overseas, the men distinguished themselves in such battles as Vimy Ridge, Ypres, the Somme and Passchendaele. Many enlisted for the fun and glory of warfare, or for free room and board and a dollar a day, only to find themselves embroiled in four years of muddy and filthy trenches, whistling shells, bloated corpses, rats and lice, poison gas, blood and death. Many of those less eager to enlist had fallen victim to volunteer recruiters who scoured the countryside for eligible soldiers to fill the fast-dwindling ranks overseas. "Be a man!" newspaper advertisements declared, "Get into khaki." Some soldiers, like Harry Leslie of Souris, were decorated for bravery, but more suffered Private William Henry Coffin's fate and were buried quietly overseas. In 1916, the 105th Highland Regiment (one-quarter of its members were "Macs") left for France, singing,

We're from Prince Edward Island,
'Tis a land of noble worth,
You'll see by our geographee
'Tis the only Island on earth.
We have water all around us,
Yet they say that we are "dry";
Oh we're the boys to raise the noise
With our regimental cry.

Making the Island Dry

The First World War aided the government's struggle to quell the liquor trade on P.E.I. The temperance movement dated back to the Island's pioneer days, when taverns dotted the countryside. Presbyterian minister Robert Patterson established the first temperance society in 1831 in Centreville (now known as Bedeque). This was followed by such organizations as the Sons of Temperance, the Independent Order of Good Templars and the Women's Christian Temperance Union. Temperance groups combined cultural and educational activities with their evangelizing, and in many rural areas the temperance society constituted the major community organization.

The temperance movement had had its ups and downs throughout the century, as "wets" fought "drys" for supremacy. The wets had defeated two attempts to pass prohibitory legislation in the late 1850s by arguing for freedom of choice and by warning voters that taxes would increase if the licensing of liquor taverns was abolished. The defeated temperance leaders gradually moved from approving moderate use of beers and wine (but not spirits) to advocating total abstinence, and from attempting to win converts by the use of moral arguments to demanding government legislation prohibiting all alcohol consumption (except that needed for sacramental and medicinal purposes). The Canada Temperance Act of 1878 allowed each municipality to decide by majority vote whether liquor could be sold within its boundaries. Except for Charlottetown, most Island communities favoured prohibition. The temperance leaders generally prevailed, and Islanders consumed considerably less liquor per person than any other province. Local prohibition, however, did not deter people from drinking. Alcohol passed easily from wet to dry areas, enforcement was weak, and moonshining became both a popular and a lucrative enterprise. (The law did not prohibit the manufacture of alcohol, just its consumption.) When Charlottetown repealed local prohibition in 1891, the provincial government responded to the resulting increase of liquor-related offences by forcing all taverns to have only one door, prohibiting them from covering their windows with curtains or screens, allowing no partitions or furniture and forbidding the sale of anything other than liquor on the premises.

The need for field crops to feed the Allied soldiers in the First World War, and the desire to create a better world at war's end, led in 1918 to the federal government's decision to prohibit the import, manufacture and sale of alcoholic beverages in Canada. The United States followed suit with its prohibition legislation in 1920.

By 1920 in Canada, the consumption and sale of alcoholic beverages were illegal. However, the American Prohibition Act forbade the sale, but not the consumption, of alcohol. Since provincial laws in Canada did not prohibit the manufacture of liquor for export, the spirits trade to the United States provided a new source of income for the depressed Maritime fishing industry. Hundreds of fishing vessels, such as the famous *Nellie J. Banks*, were refitted and used to quench American thirst. During the 1920s, every province in Canada but P.E.I. abandoned prohibition in favour of government-operated liquor stores. This situation merely provided another market for the rum runners when the United States ended prohibition in 1933. In the game of wits between the authorities and the rum runners on the Island, the latter usually won. Anchored outside the government's three-mile jurisdiction, the rum runners lured government patrols away through various stratagems and then landed their illegal cargo in one of the Island's many deserted bays or coves. Other tactics involved hiding liquor in lobster traps or attaching the illicit goods to buoys.

To help combat the rum trade and to control the increasing automobile traffic, the province created its own provincial police force in 1930. This small contingent in khaki or navy-blue uniforms patrolled rural areas, enforced the Lord's Day Act, and deported hoboes to New Brunswick, but they were generally unsuccessful in enforcing the less-than-popular liquor laws. In 1932, the Royal Canadian Mounted Police replaced the provincial police force. The Mounties proved no more effective than the provincial police in controlling the liquor trade, and rum running did not end until the Island government rescinded prohibition in 1948.

ELEVEN

Make room, make room!

A Time of Change

About ninety years ago, a young couple was out driving in their horse and buggy when they saw a weird contraption coming toward them. Small explosions and all sorts of rattling noises filled the air. This was the first automobile they had ever seen. The young woman and man had all they could do to control the wild-eyed horses, who reared and bolted in fear. The car sputtered and banged down the middle of the road. Its driver seemed to have no concern for the rights of horses and buggies.

Automobile traffic was one of the many changes to the Prince Edward Island way of life in the late 19th and early 20th centuries. At that time, streets were unpaved. City residents carried lanterns to light their way at night. Later, oil-burning lamps were erected at street corners. Electric lights did not come to the streets of Charlottetown until 1887. At this time, there were only eleven telephones on the entire Island. Those people wanting to use the telephone turned a crank and asked an operator to ring the other party.

When the soldiers returned from the First World War, plenty of surprises awaited them. Automobiles now carefully manoeuvered their way around the ruts in the clay streets; women voted in federal elections and worked in a greater variety of jobs; alcoholic beverages were more difficult to obtain; and income tax was now a way of life. There were serious concerns about the high inflation rate; an onslaught of Spanish Flu, which claimed as many Canadian lives as had the war; and growing unemployment as war industries shut down. Against this backdrop of technological progress, new social and political conditions and an uncertain economy came changes in the ways Islanders communicated among themselves and with the outside world.

Crossing the Strait

The first permanent steamboat connection between the Island and the mainland began in 1842. The boats, owned by the P.E.I. Steam Navigation Company, visited Pictou, Nova Scotia; Charlottetown; Bedeque; Georgetown; and Miramichi, New Brunswick, every two weeks. However, service was expensive and the boats were never on time.

The Island had agreed to Confederation in 1873 partly because of Canada's promise to provide "efficient and continuous communication" between the Island and the mainland. The first ferry provided by the Canadian government was the *Albert* (1875). It was made mostly of wood and couldn't break through the thick winter ice. Although the next steamboat, the *Northern Light* (1876), was steel hulled, it also was not strong enough to fight the heavy winter ice, and averaged only twenty-one round trips a winter. The *Stanley* (1888) was a big improvement. This steel icebreaker made an average of seventy-nine round trips each winter, yet even the *Stanley* was subject to the perils of harsh weather. In 1890, for example, it was unable to make the crossing for forty-three consecutive days. The *Minto* (1899) could cut through 28 centimetres (11 inches) of solid ice; if the ice was thicker than this, the *Minto* was driven onto the ice to crush it with the boat's weight. If the ice still did not break, the ship became stranded and the passengers were forced to walk to the nearest shore.

From 1827 to 1918, small ice boats were used to transport mail across the Northumberland Strait. An ice boat was usually 5 metres (16.5 feet) long and 1.2 metres (4 feet) wide, and was covered with tin to protect the boat from the grinding ice. Some of these boats had long metal runners on both sides of the keel. Depending upon the weather, the crews of ice boats used sails, oars or paddles to cross the Strait. When the ice became too thick, the men pulled the boats over the ice on the metal runners. The crews were attached to the ice boats by long leather harnesses that went over the shoulder and around the waist. The harnesses were used to pull the boats over the ice and snow, and they saved the men from drowning if the ice gave way.

Crossing Northumberland Strait by Ice Boat

Prince Edward Island is separated from the mainland by masses of moving ice for nearly five months each year. In 1827, a weekly winter ferry connection was established between Cape Traverse and Cape Tormentine. The boats were sailed, rowed or dragged by the captain, a coxswain, four crew members and those passengers who wished to pay a reduced fare in exchange for their help.

A difficult crossing

The first ice boats were poorly equipped. After an accident in 1885, in which several men were lost for two days and almost died, each boat was required to carry a compass, two extra paddles, food and the means to make a fire. The men who worked on the ice boats were chosen for their strength and endurance. While those who worked the ice boats were brave and sturdy, just as brave — or as foolhardy — were the passengers who made the dangerous crossing. The rates were two dollars for women; four dollars for men who wished to remain in the boat; and two dollars for men who helped push or pull the boat across the ice. With luck, a crossing took only three-and-a-half hours. Sometimes, however, the boats became stuck in the ice and the passengers had to walk to shore. In 1843, ten people were lost in the strait for two days; twelve years later, two men died during a crossing.

To provide for safer and more regular traffic, some Islanders tried to persuade the Canadian government to build a tunnel under Northumberland Strait. This idea was popular from 1884 to 1914. The first plan was to build an iron tube along the bottom of the Strait. The enormous amount of money involved and the complex engineering problems prevented the construction of such a tunnel. The demand for a tunnel died down after the *Prince Edward Island*, the first ferry capable of carrying railway cars and automobiles, was built in 1918. In later years, ferries were improved and enlarged. The *Charlottetown* could carry forty-one automobiles; the *Abegweit*, sixty-nine. The latter vessel now serves as the clubhouse of the Columbia Yacht Club on Lake Michigan. In 1982, *Abegweit II* came on-stream. Affectionately known as "The Abby," it was retired only when the Confederation Bridge opened in 1997. It had a capacity of 974 passengers, 20 railway cars and 250 automobiles.

Despite these improvements, ferry service remained slow. At Wood Islands, Northumberland Ferries Inc. began ferry services to and from Pictou, Nova Scotia, in the 1950s, and has continued to do so from April to December, although it is uncertain whether there will be sufficient traffic and federal government subsidies to keep this service operating. The idea of constructing a bridge or causeway from the Island to the mainland was discussed in the 1960s. Although a start was made, the idea was abandoned in 1969 in favour of $225 million over the next fifteen years toward a development plan for the Island. As discussed in the final chapter, interest in a fixed link was to emerge again in the 1980s.

The Arrival of the Automobile

Father Georges-Antoine Belcourt shocked the people of Rustico in 1866 when he drove a "horseless carriage" to the community's annual picnic. This was the first automobile operated in Canada! Early cars were not very practical. They kept breaking down and were very expensive. By 1907, there were only seven automobiles in the province, but people were curious enough about these new-fangled horseless carriages to pay a dime for an automobile ride at fairs and picnics, or to take pictures of friends sitting in the front seat.

Islanders not only loved their horses, but also relied on them to transport their produce to market. Horses were often terrified by automobiles, and there were several accidents involving automobiles and horses. Worse, there was speculation that cars would eventually replace horses. Many Islanders didn't want this to happen, especially since only wealthy people could afford horseless carriages. Some people complained that many farmers stayed home on market days and that people didn't attend church for fear of meeting an automobile. In 1908, the government banned automobiles from Prince Edward Island. The sentence for anyone caught driving a car was six months in jail or a fine of $500.

In 1913, cars were allowed to operate on Mondays, Wednesdays and Thursdays, but only on certain roads. Each community decided whether or not it would permit automobiles. The result was instant confusion. If a car broke down on Thursday, its owner had to wait until Monday before driving it home. If an automobile owner lived

The Bicycle Craze

The development of the modern bicycle in 1885, with its diamond-shaped frame, equal-sized wheels and endless chain, and the adoption of pneumatic tires three years later, began a bicycle craze in North America. The new cycle provided cheap transportation. Telegraph boys sped down the road to deliver messages. Doctors rode bicycles on house calls. Chaperones were among the first casualties, and waist-pinching corsets and multi-layered petticoats with their whalebone stiffeners were not far behind. Although there were no velodromes in Prince Edward Island, bicycle road racing was very popular. The *Patriot* provides the following description of such a race:

> As usual, accidents were quite common. Mr. Moore collided with a cow, which injured the fork of his wheel and impeded his speed afterwards. Mr. Haszard was unfortunate to break his handle-bars before leaving and had to borrow one. Mr. Duchemin when coming down the first hill struck a stone and was thrown from his wheel and rendered unable to take any further active part in the race ... Afterwards, there was an ice-cream and strawberry banquet, followed by speeches and a feast.

in an area that prohibited cars, the owner had to pull the car by horse to an area that allowed them. Some farmers continued to object to automobiles and blockaded roads to prevent automobile traffic.

All restrictive automobile legislation was finally removed in 1918. Still, it took a while before everyone became used to this form of transportation. Children amused themselves by writing down the licence numbers of cars that went by and hurried home to look in car registration books to see where the drivers lived. Lucy Maud Montgomery had mixed feelings about the automobile coming to the Island. "In one way I'm rather pleased," she wrote, "I hate to hear the Island made fun of for its prejudice against cars. On the other hand I resent their presence, I wanted to think that there was one place in the world where the strident honk-honk of a car-horn could never jar on the scented air."

Since early cars had no windshields, dust was a problem on unpaved Island roads. Women often wore veils and long coats called "dusters" to protect their clothes. Flat tires were a common occurrence. The motorist had to take off the tire, remove the inner tube, patch it, push the inner tube back into the tire and then put the tire back on the wheel. Many roads were too narrow to allow cars to pass one another, and a driver might be forced to back up half a mile before there was enough room for another car to pass. The first paved road on the Island was not finished until 1934.

Some early-model cars possessed oil lights that had to be lighted by hand and engines that required cranking. Until 1924, cars drove on the left-hand side of the road. P.E.I. was behind the other provinces in accepting the automobile: in 1921, for example, the Island had one car for every fifty-three people, compared with the national average of one for every twenty-eight. By 1931, however, the Island had narrowed the gap to one car for every thirteen people, whereas the national average was one for every ten people.

The automobile revolutionized all aspects of Island life. By the 1920s it had moved from being a luxury to a necessity. The average Canadian selling price dropped from $900 in 1921 to $700 five years later. As car registrations increased, so did road building, service stations and traffic signs.

Radio Broadcasting

Communication was not just a matter of improved travel over Island roads or across the Strait. With the development of radio, Islanders received instant news from around the world. Keith S. Rogers, a prominent Island pioneer in the development of radio, was born in Summerside in 1892. He was fascinated by telegraphy, and at age fifteen, built his first wireless set in the bathroom of his parents' home. The method of transmitting messages at this time was the "dot dash," or Morse code, system. Keith taught his girlfriend (later his wife) Morse code and installed a wireless set in her home so that they could communicate whenever they wished. In 1922, there were only fifty to one hundred Island homes with radio receivers. By this time, Rogers was broadcasting noon and evening programs from his living room. Later, working with Walter E. Burke, he broadcast from various locations in Charlottetown.

A group of amateurs, including Walter Burke, Walter Hyndman and Keith Rogers, organized the Radio Club of Charlottetown in 1922. In the spring of 1923, their experimental station 10AS began broadcasting from 3:30 p.m. to 4:45 p.m. Three years later, R. T. Holman opened a station — CHGS — in his Summerside store. At this time, Prince Edward Island had two radio stations, New Brunswick had two and Nova Scotia only one. In 1928, Walter Burke opened CHCK in Charlottetown, which lasted until the start of the Second World War. At the time of his death in 1954, Keith Rogers was planning the first television station on the Island. This project was continued by his son-in-law, R. F. Large, and the first television program was broadcast in 1956.

TWELVE

Soldiers, by Robert Harris

The Depression and the Second World War

General dissatisfaction with the gradual decline of the Maritime economy in the first three decades of the century led to the creation of the Maritime Rights Movement. Its proponents sought to use regional cooperation to force the federal government to respond to the area's economic problems. In particular, they sought lower tariffs, larger federal subsidies and reduced freight rates (which had increased by as much as 200 percent following the First World War). Prince Edward Island was less affected by the regional economic malaise than were Nova Scotia and New Brunswick. As a result, Maritime Rights never became a major political issue, and the Island was "bought off" by a Royal Commission and offers of larger federal subsidies and a new car ferry.

Despite the prevailing view that the Maritimes survived the Great Depression of the 1930s with less difficulty than the rest of Canada, the area was particularly hard hit. Although the Island did not experience the perils of drought and grasshoppers that destroyed the western provinces' crops, the precipitous fall in farm and fish prices nonetheless brought ruin to many families. Letters written to Prime Minister R. B. Bennett requesting financial aid described animals slowly starving to death in their stalls, children suffering from malnutrition and as much as 20 percent of the labour force unemployed. Although prices for farm produce began to improve in 1936, many farmers had no money left for seeds or fertilizer and the land had deteriorated. To make matters worse, the cost of farm machinery and manufactured goods had increased at a much faster rate than had agricultural prices.

Destitution was particularly evident in Charlottetown. Rural families could at least feed themselves. Urban dwellers, however, had to earn money to buy food and their situation was particularly precarious. Since the Island's economy revolved around farming, neither the provincial government nor the majority of the populace had much sympathy for industrial workers. Throughout the 1930s, P.E.I. was the only province that had no legislation regarding hours of work, minimum wage, factory inspection for health and safety conditions, workers' compensation, and (with Ontario) did not recognize the workers' rights to collective bargaining.

The following statistics indicate the extent of the depression. The cost of eggs declined from 30¢ a dozen to just 8¢. Cod sold for less than 1¢ a pound and lobsters for 4¢. Silver fox pelts dropped from $100 to $28 apiece. Swine declined from 16¢ to 3¢ a pound. And the price of potatoes, which also suffered from a British embargo on Canadian potatoes for fear of contamination from the Colorado beetle, sank from $1.50 to 6¢ for 100 pounds. Agricultural income thus decreased from $9.8 million in 1927 to $2.3 million five years later. The Island's $146 average income per person in 1932 was the lowest in the country. The Canadian average income was $287.

The scramble to catch skunks indicated the seriousness of the situation. Prior to the depression, a New Annan firm had sought to raise skunks for their pelts. When the public showed no interest, the farm set the forty animals free. The skunks adapted so well to the Island that the government offered a 50¢ bounty per snout to control their swelling numbers. During the depression, skunks were eagerly sought, and some people apparently bootlegged snouts from the mainland. One imaginative person manufactured snouts from cow hide. Within three years, the government had paid bounties on more than fifteen thousand skunk snouts.

The provincial Conservative Party was one of the first casualties of the hard times. Although the depression was no one's fault, the Liberals under Walter Lea swept all thirty seats in the 1935 election — a Canadian first. A new party in power, however, did not mean a new approach to the problem. With limited financial resources, the government was reluctant to adopt social welfare policies, and P.E.I. was one of the last provinces to provide old-age pensions and mother's allowance. In 1933, the government bowed to public pressures and paid pensions to those seventy years of age or over. It set the maximum pension at $15, established a strict means test and made it mandatory for children to support their parents.

Because federal relief programs were administered on a matching grants formula, P.E.I. received less money per capita than the wealthier provinces, further hampering industrial development.

Public works programs were more attractive objects for government spending. In the 1930s, the unemployed built bridges and wharves, paved the Trans-Canada Highway and remodelled public buildings. In Summerside, workers constructed a sea wall and a municipal airport, paved the streets, and improved the water and sewage systems. As a result of such activities, the provincial government expanded its bureaucracy and was forced by the circumstances to take responsibility for the welfare of the people.

The 1930s were not entirely without their good times. Many people fondly remember this period for its camaraderie, as communities cooperated to help the needy. Parties held at a poor person's home broke up early, leaving enough leftover food for the rest of the week. "Bees" provided entertainment and financed such useful tasks as haying and ploughing. To help the drought-stricken western Canadian farmers, Islanders sent sixty box-car loads of agricultural produce. This act of generosity, declared one relief official, should be "chronicled as one of the most inspirational gestures in Canadian history. Certainly, if Canadianism means anything, this means a great deal in the shaping of a true and loyal national consciousness."

Conveniences in 1941

Percentage of homes with:

	Radio	Phone	Electric Vacuum	Car
P.E.I.	60	22	6	29
N.S.	73	33	16	28
N.B.	65	27	12	26
CANADA	78	40	24	37

Percentage of farm homes with:

	Electric Light	Running Water	Flush Toilet	Bathtub
P.E.I.	6	9	6	7
N.S.	26	14	9	10
N.B.	19	13	8	7
CANADA	20	12	9	7

Co-operatives

When American professor John T. Croteau drove into the village of North Rustico in 1933, he found it "sunken in misery — a collection of unpainted fishermen's shacks, a falling-down, cold school building, so old that no one remembered when it had been built, and a little mission church. Incomes were below subsistence level. During the winter months many families existed on one or two scanty meals a day ... It was a picture of misery and despair." When Croteau returned twelve years later, he observed that the community was now prosperous thanks to the activities of resident pastor Father Douglas MacNeil. "Study clubs were organized. A credit union was formed. A fishermen's union was incorporated and a co-operative lobster factory built. Later a co-operative store was started. As conditions improved the people of the community bought an unused warehouse, hauled it to a new site and converted it into a modern school ... There is a library in the building and radios in every classroom ... The church was extended to more than twice the size of the old one. A paved road was built through the village and electric lights extended through the town."

Co-operative ventures were not new on the Island. Father Georges-Antoine Belcourt had created the Farmers' Bank of Rustico in 1864, and later established grain banks to loan seeds to Acadian farmers. Across the province, farmers had formed co-operatives to process and market their goods. By 1931, the Prince Edward Island Co-operative Egg and Poultry Association had 3,800 members; the Potato Growers' Association helped purchase fertilizers, standardize grades, eradicate disease and market farmers' crops. Tignish fishers had organized their own union in 1923, and two years later began operating a lobster cannery.

Co-operative ventures quickly multiplied during the depression. The spark behind their growth was provided by Dr. Moses Coady of St. Francis Xavier University in Antigonish, Nova Scotia. Coady was the founder of the Antigonish Movement, which sought to make common people "masters of their own destiny." Copying his methods, Islanders formed credit unions and co-operative stores, and established marketing and warehousing organizations.

PEIPARO

The smallest chartered bank in Canada

Coady was also interested in adult education, and, in 1933, Professor Croteau applied the Antigonish adult education program to Prince Edward Island. Working with the extension service at St. Dunstan's University, Croteau helped form study groups throughout the province. They raised money and provided entertainment by sponsoring dances, card games and socials. They examined the major economic problems of the day, and they taught the people how to organize and operate credit unions, co-operative stores, unions and community projects. Tignish led the way. Co-operative ventures provided health care, financial loans, groceries, automobile service, fish processing and marketing services for Irish Moss, blueberries and other produce. Although the co-operative movement declined across the Island in the 1950s, it remains strong in western Prince County.

War Again

The Second World War was a time of tragedy. More than 50 million people died, including 42,000 Canadians. Almost 9,000 Islanders volunteered for overseas service, the highest volunteer-to-population ratio of any province in the country.

The war ended the depression. By 1941 there were enough jobs for all who wanted them, and the demand had increased for agricultural and fishing products. Lobster and fish prices skyrocketed. Hake and mackerel, rich in proteins, were canned and sold to an international organization that supplied food to victims of the war. The loss of the Japanese supply of agar, after Pearl Harbor in 1941, led to the collection of Irish Moss for use as a food additive and gelling product.

The threat of invasion from the skies led to a series of practice blackouts, during which all indoor lights were shielded from outside view. Over forty air-raid sirens were erected in various centres across the Island. Naval attacks, however, were more likely to occur. In May of 1942, a German submarine torpedoed a British steamer near Anticosti Island in the Gulf of St. Lawrence. Later that year, the H.M.C.S. *Charlottetown* was torpedoed, struck a reef and sank off the Nova Scotia coast. The following year, the Newfoundland ferry, the *Caribou*, went down in the Gulf of St. Lawrence.

When Prime Minister W. L. M. King agreed to take part in the British Commonwealth Air Training Program for Allied pilots, Canada had to select suitable sites. Fortunately for P.E.I., Canada's minister of defence, R. L. Ralston, had lost his bid for election in 1935. In desperation, Ralston persuaded the Prince County Liberal Association to allow him to run there in a by-election. The victorious Ralston rewarded his adopted constituency with military bases at Mount Pleasant, Wellington and St. Eleanors, which created immediate prosperity in Prince County. The Mount Pleasant base became an air-gunnery school, where the men practised shooting ink-coloured bullets at a white silk target pulled behind an aircraft. Although the training school employed a large civilian staff and was of major economic and social importance to western Prince County, Ottawa closed the airport at the conclusion of the war. A

Carl Burke and the History of Aviation on P.E.I.

The history of flying in Prince Edward Island began in 1912, when a young Cuban pilot flew a homemade plane over the Exhibition Grounds in Charlottetown. But it was not until 1941, when Carl Burke founded Maritime Central Airways, that Prince Edward Island became important in the aviation history of Canada.

Carl Frederick Burke was born in Charlottetown in 1913. When he was a young boy, his greatest dream was to fly a plane. In 1937, his dream came true. While working as a hardware clerk for R. T. Holman, he saved enough money from his $12 weekly salary to take flying lessons for $10 per hour. That same year, Burke bought his first plane, a D. H. Cirrus Moth, and he and his aircraft soon became a familiar sight in Island skies.

In 1939, after earning his commercial pilot's licence, Carl Burke became a pilot with Canadian Airways. During the Second World War, he flew planes from Canada to England. At this time, Burke and his friend, Joe Anderson, made plans to start their own air service for the Maritime provinces. Although Joe Anderson was killed in a plane crash a few months later, Maritime Central Airways of Charlottetown made its first flight in 1941. By 1963, when Carl Burke sold the airline to Eastern Provincial Airways, M.C.A. had become Canada's largest independent cargo airline.

similar fate befell the emergency landing strip at Wellington, the search and rescue station at Alberton South and the radar base at Tignish.

The St. Eleanors base, which served as a flying school and later as a reconnaissance school, remained after the war and quickly assumed a vital economic role in the area. Local Summerside merchants found a ready market for their goods at the base, and civilians secured employment there. After the Island successfully resisted two attempts in the 1960s and 1970s to close the base, the federal government (which lost all four Island seats in the 1988 election) shut down CFB Summerside in 1989. Since the base had been the second largest employer on P.E.I. and had pumped about $50 million into the economy annually, Summerside — the second-largest town in the province — faced difficult economic decisions. With considerable local and provincial assistance, an aircraft manufacturing plant and other businesses moved to the former air base. In response to public pressure over the decision to close the base, the federal government established a Goods and Services Tax (GST) branch in Summerside.

Despite the boost given to the economy by the Second World War, at war's end the Maritimes were still the underprivileged region of the country. Following the Second World War, the average income per person was about two-thirds the national average, and the region's unemployment rate was more than double the Canadian average. The region had the highest rates of illiteracy, infant mortality and tuberculosis in Canada and was heavily dependent upon primary-sector industries, in which employment was often seasonal. At the urging of Maritime politicians and business people, in the late 1950s the federal government took measures to reduce regional inequalities. Beginning in 1957, the equalization program transferred money from the richer areas of Canada to poorer provinces such as P.E.I. to help them reach parity with the rest of Canada in terms of medical and educational services.

THIRTEEN

There was a home remedy for every ill

Caring for the Sick

Pioneer Doctoring

In October 1821, Doctor John Mackieson boarded the brig *Relief* and arrived in Charlottetown after a relatively short, thirty-six-day voyage. Little is known about John Mackieson's life before he came to Prince Edward Island, apart from the facts that he was born in Scotland in 1795, received a classical education before beginning a study of medicine at the University of Glasgow, and that upon graduation in 1815, he was employed by the Faculty of Physicians & Surgeons of Glasgow "to exercise the Arts of Surgery and Pharmacy."

The primitive nature of Prince Edward Island must have surprised the young doctor, who settled in the Island's capital (spelled Charlotte Town until incorporation in 1855). When Mackieson arrived in the colony, the roads were still so rudimentary that few four-wheeled carriages were available, and all travel was by foot or horse. The narrow roads between settlements were virtually impassable in the winter, when the strong winds created huge snow drifts. In the spring and fall, the heavy red mud turned the rutted roads into knee-deep quagmires. Because the doctor had an extensive practice throughout Queens County, the weather and the condition of the roads were a constant concern. As late as 1856, he noted in his diary with pride that it took him only three hours over deeply drifted roads to travel the twenty miles to New Glasgow, and in November 1861 another trip to New Glasgow consumed three and a half hours because the trail was "like walking through liquid mud."

For most Islanders, these early pioneer years were a continuous struggle to survive. In such primitive conditions, the difference between life and death might depend on how quickly the doctor could attend the patient. In 1834, for example, Doctor Mackieson received an urgent message to come to St. Peters to treat a strangulated hernia. Since it was a thirty-mile trip, the physician did not arrive until late in the evening, and he had to operate by candlelight. Six years later, Alexander Nicholson of Murray Harbour dislocated and severely gashed his leg in the woods. Only his wife and mother were present to provide medical assistance, and he suffered for several days before they could bring him to Charlottetown. By then it was too late for Alexander, who had died from his infected wounds, and almost too late for his wife, who delivered twins shortly after her arrival in Charlottetown.

The pioneer conditions attracted few doctors. The distance between the small settlements necessitated constant travel, while the settlers' poverty meant that most patients paid their medical bills in farm produce. When Mackieson arrived on Prince Edward Island there were only a few doctors in the colony. Many people preferred to rely on home remedies and patent medicines or call on a trusted neighbour rather than incur the costs of a physician's visit.

At this time, Prince Edward Island had no hospital, no public health legislation and fewer than a dozen physicians. When an outbreak of typhus fever was reported in New Brunswick in 1827, the Island enacted its first public health bill and closed Charlottetown to all infected incoming vessels. The harbour master stopped all ships at the mouth of the harbour until the newly appointed government health officer had inspected each passenger. Once the threat had passed, however, the law was allowed to lapse. Charlottetown remained without a hospital until 1879. Even then, the hospital's charter prohibited the admittance of patients with contagious diseases. At each threat of contagion, the board of health rented a small house for the infected patients and later had it burned to the ground.

As Charlottetown grew in size and importance and the Island population expanded, Mackieson's practice and status also increased. Following the custom of the other physicians in town, John Mackieson had advertised his arrival in the newspaper. By 1836, Mackieson's practice had expanded so much that he could advertise in the newspaper for "a young man of character and education" interested in being his apprentice and studying to become a physician.

By today's standards, the doctor's office was extremely primitive. For example, in January 1837, a man arrived at Mackieson's doorstep with his sick wife after an eight-hour sleigh trip. While the doctor was examining the wife, she became so faint and exhausted that she had to lie down for half an hour on the carpet, while her husband agonized over whether he could reach home with her alive. The apparent lack of even a bed might be explained by the fact that most people preferred to be examined in their own homes, and a visit to the physician's office was regarded as a mark of lower status.

Doctors sought to help their patients as best they could, but early nineteenth-century medical knowledge had little chance of success. Physicians knew nothing of the role of bacteria or viruses in disease, and therefore lacked even the most rudimentary understanding of infection and the need for sterilization. Surgery was often fatal and was limited to setting fractures, lancing boils, operating on strangulated hernias and performing amputations. The inability of physicians to make accurate diagnoses prevented them from scientifically testing the validity of their therapies.

Therapy was a matter of regulating or altering the patients' symptoms, which were not regarded as signs of the disease, but as the disease itself. The physician's art centred on his ability to employ appropriate drugs to produce particular physiological effects. Opium calmed the patient and reduced body temperature; alcohol quickened weak heart rates; mercury produced diarrhea and salivation; bloodletting altered the pulse and removed "bad blood" from the body.

John Mackieson's medical practices were no different from those of other physicians at the time. He diligently recorded the rate of each patient's pulse; the temperature, colour and texture of the skin; the length of sleep; the colour of the blood; and the quantity, smell and characteristics of the urine, sputum and faeces. These signs not only shed light on the body's internal state, but also provided day-to-day indicators of the patient's reactions to the medicines. To cleanse the stomach and bowels, Mackieson employed emetics to induce violent vomiting and purgatives to act as powerful laxatives. Once the system was cleansed, he used such tonics or stimulants as arsenic, laudanum and alcohol to restore the system by improving the appetite. Doctor Mackieson recommended spice wine, brandy and liqueur brandies to restore "drooping strength," "elevate the animal spirits," and cure "exhaustion, faintness, depressions, grief, cramps, and gouty spasms of the stomach and bowels."

Mackieson used bloodletting, or leeching, for almost every malady. Rapid fluid loss lowered body temperature and reduced the pulse rate. Although the drugs employed by the medical profession seem cruel and dangerous today, the physicians believed in the therapeutics they practised. When Mackieson contracted typhus fever, he took wine and other stimulants, was blistered on the back of his neck, and applied mustard poultices to the bottoms of his feet. Later, he ate chicken and mutton soups with brown toast to restore his health.

John Mackieson was particularly proficient with the scalpel, and assisted other physicians with strangulated hernias and compound fractures. The difficulty of performing amputations without anaesthetic usually meant that several physicians cooperated. Since physicians lacked a knowledge of germs and the need for sterile conditions, open wounds were often fatal, and surgery was a high-risk procedure. In 1845, when a man's broken leg became gangrenous, Mackieson agonized about the proper course of action. "It now became necessary to decide on an operation," he recorded in his *Sketches*, "to leave him to his fate he might live 48 hours ... but the question was would an amputation save him, I resolved to give him the chance by amputation, it was performed by myself, assisted by Dr. Tremaine & Mr. Cook surgeon."

Disease, accidents and death were common occurrences during Mackieson's lifetime. In his own family, his youngest son, Augustus, died at age twenty-eight after a long illness. A son-in-law also passed away in the prime of his life in 1863. A grandson lived only eight months, a granddaughter died of diarrhea at seven months and another granddaughter lived only three years. Other pioneer families had similar tales to tell. Chief Justice Edward Jarvis, for instance, survived two wives and five children. His first wife, Anna, gave birth to eight children, three of whom died in infancy and one in childhood. He had three offspring with his second wife, Elizabeth, one of whom died shortly after delivery. Elizabeth died giving birth to their third child.

Childbirth was the central event in most women's lives. At mid-century, the average woman gave birth to approximately seven children. Although rickets, poor nutrition and unsanitary conditions resulted in a high infant mortality rate, most births were successful. Every women knew, however, that childbirth could be fatal, and one of the first choices a pregnant woman had to make was who would deliver her child. In most isolated areas in Prince Edward Island, there were few choices. Since doctors were expensive and not always accessible, the woman naturally turned to her mother, aunt, sister, female friend or midwife for help. Unlike the doctor, these women provided emotional support throughout the entire nine months and helped with the household chores.

Mackieson rarely made either pre- or post-natal visits. He was summoned only after labour had commenced or when complications arose. He sometimes remained all night, or even several days, but usually departed after the birth. Although Mackieson rarely used forceps, sometimes he had no choice. In January 1856, John Tetsen summoned Dr. Mackieson to attend his pregnant wife. She was just twenty years old, and this was to be their first child. Upon arrival, the physician immediately assumed control from the midwife. Since Mrs. Tetsen had been in labour for more than eighteen hours, Dr. Mackieson gave her two doses of ergot to promote abdominal contractions. The drug caused severe discomfort and induced full labour pains, but the child's head lodged against the pubic bone and Mackieson could not free it. Fearing for the mother's health if labour continued much longer, the physician removed his forceps from his medical bag and placed the unsterilized tool around the baby's head. Since the child was firmly lodged against the bone, Dr. Mackieson had to pull with all his strength. After a little over two hours of medical attendance, the mother delivered a baby boy. Sadly, the child died within the week. Mackieson listed the reason for this death in his medical log as "cause unknown."

Early Dentistry

During the nineteenth century, dentistry was largely an itinerant profession. Since restorative procedures were expensive and most dental work consisted mainly of extraction, few communities had the full-time services of a trained dentist. In the first half of the century, dentists' activities were confined to the alleviation of pain. A typical advertisement in the Charlottetown *Examiner* read:

> *Dr. Shaw, Dentist, Has arrived in town and taken rooms at the Victoria Hotel, where he will remain for a limited period. Those wishing his services are requested to give him an early call. Ladies waited on at their residence if required.*

In the second half of the century, the use of ether as a general anaesthetic and the adoption of materials such as silver amalgam, gold foil and later vulcanite, allowed dentists to fill cavities and restore diseased teeth. Dentists also provided collections of artificial teeth. In 1890, for example, J. A. Stackhouse offered the "best sets of teeth, Canadian, American, or English-made, mounted on red, black, or maroon vulcanite rubber bases for $8.00." Since most dentists' offices lacked electricity, the patient sat facing the window for better visibility.

In an age when medicine and dentistry were poorly understood, many people could be easily taken advantage of by unscrupulous hucksters who offered their services, complete with entertainment, in the town square. When "Professor Ashley" arrived in Charlottetown from Montreal in 1880, his publicist announced:

> *The King of Dentists will perform on his Electro instruments unknown to any one. His wonderful operation in Public FREE. Positively no fear of pain.*

> *The Professor can be consulted on all kinds of diseases, rheumatism, liver complaint, bronchial affection, catarrh, deafness, sore eyes, kidney complaints, colic, cramps, fits, cuts, sores, bruises, and all kinds of weaknesses, also cures stiffness of the joints, muscles, and sprains, and cancers can be removed by drawing.*

> *The professor will appear in Market Hall commencing on Wednesday evening the 21st instant for one week or more, with a pleasing Specialty Company — Everything new and original. Don't forget to attend the Entertainment and enjoy*

a good hearty laugh. A grand Exhibition of Teeth Extracting will be given after each performance by the Professor and Mrs. Ashley the Queen of Dentists.

This is your only chance — Don't fail to attend and see the Crowned Queen.

When one patient haemorrhaged after the "professor" had extracted her molar, the King of Dentists quietly skipped town before the patient's husband could collect damages.

The Red Cross

Throughout the nineteenth and early twentieth centuries, in the absence of government help, Islanders took care of their own sick and mentally and physically challenged family members. Churches and such volunteer organizations as the Charlottetown Tuberculosis Society and the Canadian Red Cross Society provided additional assistance. Although most Islanders believed that P.E.I.'s rural environment was healthful, the state of the people's health was especially poor.

This was particularly evident in the schools, which were themselves in deplorable condition. In 1913, for example, the Chief Superintendent of Education wrote that "some of the schoolhouses are really unfit for human habitation and will soon have to be condemned." Most one-room school houses (in 1924, 416 of the Island's 472 schools were one room) were poorly constructed and equipped. The buildings were too hot in the summer and too cold in the winter. In the winter, students sitting close to the box stove were roasted, while pupils sitting at the perimeters of the room shivered. Poor ventilation and cross-lighting further hindered the pupils' education. Outhouses frequently stank and faeces littered their floors. The predominantly female teachers were underpaid and undereducated, as the better educated tended to leave the Island.

The general public did not became aware of the terrible state of the children's teeth until the Island branch of the Canadian Red Cross Society conducted medical inspections of the schools in 1921. Travelling by horse and buggy, Canadian Red Cross nurse Amy MacMahon and her assistant visited over one-third of the

Island's 480 schools and examined almost six thousand students. The nurses were shocked at the high proportion of children who had decayed teeth. In some homes there was only one family toothbrush, and those individuals who owned toothbrushes tended to use them only on Sundays and holidays. Rather than travel to town and incur dental expenses, poor families preferred to wait to have their teeth extracted rather than have the cavities filled. "From my experiences," Red Cross nurse Mona Wilson informed a class of prospective teachers in 1929, "there are many who seem to think it quite unnecessary to save teeth by having them filled, that the thing to do is to wait until they ache then go to the dentist and have them pulled — or let tooth decay progress until the poison seeps into the body causing far more serious conditions — heart and stomach trouble, shattered nerves, joint deformities, or other crippling conditions. They will shrug their shoulders and say 'Oh well, Mary will have to get false teeth.'"

Despite the nurses' efforts, subsequent inspections revealed few improvements. One of the problems was the lack of dentists. The Island had one dentist for every 4,660 people. Only Quebec had a worse population-to-dentist ratio. The fact that most of the Island's twenty-two dentists lived in either Charlottetown or Summerside partially accounted for the greater proportion of dental decay in rural children. Improvements in the students' dental health would not come until after the Second World War.

Mona Wilson: Public Health Pioneer

No one was more important to the development of public health in Prince Edward Island than Mona Wilson. After graduating from Toronto's finest schools in 1915, Mona enrolled in the nursing diploma program at The Johns Hopkins Hospital in Baltimore and later served in France with the American Army Nursing Corps during the First World War. In 1919, she joined the American Red Cross Society and departed for Siberia. By the time she left Vladivostok, Mona had experienced a failed coup attempt and had watched helplessly as mounted Bolshevik soldiers rode into her hospital ward looking for deserters.

Her next posting was in the Balkans, where she conducted home visitations; accompanied mobile clinics into the mountains; taught the benefits of fresh air, infant care and personal hygiene; initiated school inspections; and trained young women in the principles of public health nursing.

Returning to Toronto, Mona earned her Public Health Nursing Diploma and in 1923 became Chief Red Cross Public Health Nurse in Prince Edward Island. In the absence of a provincial health department, Mona conducted medical inspections in the schools, established dental clinics, Junior Red Cross clubs, tuberculosis chest clinics, crippled children's camps and organized province-wide smallpox and diphtheria vaccinations. Touring the province, she preached the necessity of planting vegetable gardens, drinking milk and eating wholesome food. Later, as Provincial Director of Public Health Nursing, Mona was instrumental in hiring provincial dental hygienists, and in establishing programs in Nutrition, and Child and Maternal Health.

During the Second World War, Mona administered to the needs of shipwrecked soldiers and sailors on the North Atlantic Run. For this work she earned the nickname "the Florence Nightingale of St. John's" and received the Order of the British Empire.

In addition to these accomplishments, this dynamic woman helped to establish the Girl Guides, the Zonta Club, the Business and Professional Women's Club, and several other Island associations that sought to broaden the people's vision and boost women's self-confidence. By the time she passed away in 1981, Mona Wilson had been awarded the highest honour in international nursing, in Girl Guides and in Prince Edward Island.

FOURTEEN

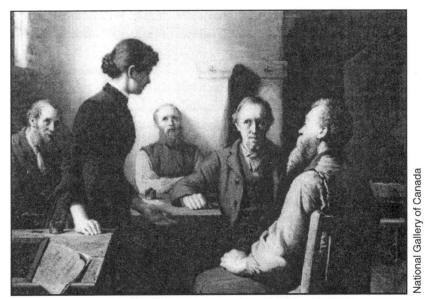

A Meeting of School Trustees, by Robert Harris

Education

Pioneer Education

Until the second half of the nineteenth century, formal education had to be paid for, and few people on the Island had either the time or the money to invest in such a luxury. Wealthy parents either sent their children to boarding schools off the Island or hired private tutors to instruct them. Many families kept their children at home to help with the house and farm work.

In 1825, the government provided a modest amount of money for each district to build a small, one-room school and hire a teacher. Due to low salaries, some teachers were forced to "board around": each week, the teacher lived with a different family in the district.

Male teachers were preferred because they were strong enough to control the older boys. One punishment they sometimes resorted to was called "the peg." Pegs were placed in the wall, and when students misbehaved, their hair was pegged to the wall, just high enough to keep the wrongdoers on tiptoe. The only written qualification teachers required was a letter from a clergyman attesting to their moral character. No wonder so many respected members of the community signed their names with an X!

Most early schoolhouses were built of logs. As many as fifty children from five to sixteen years of age crowded into one room. In summer, the building was too hot. In winter, if the school ran out of logs for the wood stove, it became so cold that classes were cancelled for the day. Older students helped younger ones with their reading, writing and arithmetic. In many schools there were no history books, maps or atlases. The Bible was often the only book available. Only one school on the Island had a library. Because

Memories of the Little White School House

Despite their size and inadequate accommodations, the little white school-houses that dotted the countryside had many advantages. Parents and teachers were seldom more than a few doors apart, everyone helped, and therefore the values of the school and the community were similar. Along with the church and the general store, the school was at the centre of each community. The following memories of Effie Campbell describe the joys of school life:

In 1909, at age seven, I began in Southwest Lot 16 with about forty other pupils. It was a one-room school with a potbelly stove for heat in the winter. It burned coal and wood. We had to haul the ashes from this stove to a pile out behind the school.

Each day it was a different student's job to carry a pail of drinking water to the school. There was no plumbing and no electricity. At night when we had concerts, we used lanterns, otherwise we just worked by the natural sunlight streaming in through the windows.

Every Friday we were allowed to use our copybooks. These books had printing on the top of each page, and we used pens dipped in ink to copy this printing in the space below. The slates we could take home but the copybooks and the pens and ink were kept up at the teacher's desk. There were also cloths for wiping off the slates. We used to chuck these cloths at each other when the teacher wasn't in the room, but somehow she always seemed to know what we were doing and who was doing it. Then one of the boys, Freeman Campbell, figured it out — she was peeking in through the keyhole in the door. So Freeman took his pocket knife and made a plug for the keyhole. It worked and she never could see what was going on after that.

For punishment we either stood in the corner or had a switch cut from a tree laid on our hands. Most of the teachers were kind-hearted and seldom used the switch, but one teacher used to switch

of these terrible conditions and the low salaries, good teachers were scarce. Some schools had to be closed because no teachers were available.

In 1839, the government tried to solve the problem of absentee-ism by arranging school vacations during planting and harvesting time — ten days in May and eleven days in October. Students attended classes in the winter from ten in the morning until three in the afternoon, and from nine to four in the summer. Monday through Friday, as well as every second Saturday, were school days. Despite these changes, poor families could not afford to pay school fees. Since women were not allowed to enter the professions or expected to engage in commerce, few girls attended secondary school, which was considered a preparatory school for higher education.

The situation improved after 1852 when the government passed the Free Education Act, which enabled all children over five years of age to attend school free of charge. The government also created a board of education to ensure that teachers were qualified. Vacations were one week in June, one week in October, and from December 24 to January 6. As a result of these reforms, the number of children who went to school doubled within two years. Unfortunately, the act did not address religious differences, which were to plague Island educational and political authorities for the next two decades. Should the Bible be authorized for use in public schools? And should Roman Catholic schools receive public funds? These were serious questions for a society that fined individuals for cutting firewood on Sunday, and was almost equally divided between Protestants (55 percent) and Roman Catholics (45 percent). Finally, in 1877, the government decreed that all public schools be non-sectarian. Teachers were permitted to open school with Scripture readings (without comments), but student attendance was optional. A series of compromises later recognized that in urban areas, specific schools would be either Protestant or Catholic, and where having two schools was not economical, teachers would be alternated along religious lines.

Modern Schools

In 1962, the average teacher's salary in the province was $2,700, compared with $4,500 in Canada as a whole. Fewer than one out of every ten teachers had completed university. There was a lack of high schools, and until the 1930s, students had to travel to Charlottetown to take Grades Eleven and Twelve.

In response to these problems, many of the Island's small schools were closed, and replaced with larger schools, which had libraries, gymnasiums and modern facilities. The number of one-room schools was reduced from 470 in 1960 to 57 in 1972. In step with the rest of Canada, teachers' salaries and their level of education improved. More students now went beyond Grade Eight. A disadvantage of school consolidation was that many children had to be bused to school, and the community was often separated from the school system. In 1994, the number of school boards was reduced from five to three, including a French-language school board.

Higher Education

Higher education began in Prince Edward Island during the 1830s with the establishment of the non-sectarian Central Academy and the Roman Catholic St. Andrew's. Later, as the Prince of Wales College and St. Dunstan's College, these two institutions developed different educational philosophies. Prince of Wales College dedicated its efforts to producing students trained in the classics and emphasized high academic standards. St. Dunstan's combined Christian ideals with social action and extended its activities into the community.

During the 1960s, the provincial government wrestled with the contentious subject of university amalgamation. Various groups supported either separate universities, amalgamation or closer cooperation. The major debate was between the supporters of a single public institution, who believed it would help end denominational strife and religious intolerance on the Island, and the proponents of the status quo, who preferred to maintain the two distinct educational philosophies that had become a part of the Island's cultural heritage. In 1969, the provincial government united the two colleges into the non-denominational University of Prince Edward Island, which moved into St. Dunstan's buildings on its present site. The student population at U.P.E.I., especially with the addition of the Atlantic Veterinary College in 1986, has continued to increase, reaching almost three thousand in 1998.

Holland College began on the original Prince of Wales campus in downtown Charlottetown in 1969 with no traditions, but soon created an individual role for itself by offering training in practical, job-oriented subjects. It now has more than four thousand students in several campuses throughout the Island, and operates the provincial vocational high school program, the Atlantic Police

Academy, the Culinary Institute of Canada, a paramedics training course, vocational trade training, a language school and adult night classes.

FIFTEEN

Ice racing in the 1800s

CCAGM

Entertainment

In the nineteenth century, each community provided its own entertainment. Strawberry festivals, basket socials, ice-cream parties and special speakers were often combined with such serious matters as political meetings and charity fundraising. Such events were usually accompanied by the local band. In 1890, for example, the Souris Benevolent Irish Society held a fundraising tea party that promised good food, games, bowling, swings, hurdles, races and a lecture by Professor Shuttleworth on scientific farming.

Music

Music-makers were valued members of a community. In the evenings, the early settlers sang and danced to the music of the bagpipes, fiddle, mouth organ, accordion or jew's-harp. At first, music-making consisted mostly of singing or fiddling, though some religious denominations considered the fiddle a tool of the devil. There were usually very few other instruments. Most communities had their own church choirs. Two of the Island's best-known songwriters were Lawrence Doyle and Larry Gorman.

Lawrence Doyle was born near Fortune Pond in 1847. When Lawrence was a teenager, his father died and he was left to help his mother and two sisters with the family farm. Lawrence stopped school after Grade Six. Through hard work and intelligence, he became a prosperous farmer. He was also a good carpenter, an active churchman, a school trustee, a postmaster and an amateur veterinarian. It was his songwriting talent, however, that made him famous. One old-timer recounted how Doyle used to compose new songs:

He was a farmer, but in the wintertime he'd work in the shop making frames, windows and doors. My father was there; he boarded there, and he taught in the school. He'd be in the shop with Lawrence on Saturdays hanging around talking to him, and watching. He said you'd see a smile appearing on his face, you know, and then he'd walk over and take his pencil; he had a little book on his workbench, and he'd write some. Then he'd go back and be working away and by and by you'd see him smiling again and then he'd go and write a little more. And he was making up a song all the time, you know. And that's the way he used to work.

During the mid-1800s, orchestras and brass bands became popular. Before the invention of radio and television, bands, fiddle contests and step-dancing competitions were some of the most favoured forms of entertainment on the Island. Fiddling served an important function in the community. To raise money for the teacher's salary or some other worthy cause, a fiddle dance was organized and everyone was invited.

Music is still greatly appreciated. People enjoy a wide range of musical styles — classical, jazz, swing, blues, folk, traditional, rock and roll, punk, new wave and many others. Traditional Highland dancing, fiddling, square dancing and ceilidhs still survive and continue to be popular. Old-time fiddling is a lively blend of Scottish, Irish and Acadian elements. A few well-known Island musicians are Angèle Arsenault of Abram's Village, Stompin' Tom Connors of Skinners' Pond, Lennie Gallant of South Rustico, Nancy White and Richard Wood, a young fiddling sensation.

Literature

The Island has produced several famous writers. Lucy Maud Montgomery and Sir Andrew Macphail both wrote about rural Prince Edward Island, and the late Milton Acorn, Lesley-Anne Bourne, Elaine Harrison, Frank Ledwell, Richard Lemm, Joseph Sherman and John Smith have expressed their ideas about life in poetic form.

Prince Edward Isle, Adieu

The songs that people such as Lawrence Doyle and Larry Gorman wrote tell us a great deal about their lives, their communities and the times in which they lived. Their song "Prince Edward Isle, Adieu" provides a glimpse of Island history:

Come all ye hardy sons of toil,
pray lend an ear to me.
'Til I relate the stressful state
of this our country.
I will not pause to name the cause,
but keep it close in view.
Our comrades dear have got to leave
and bid this Isle adieu.

There is a band within this land
We live in pomp and pride;
To swell their store they rob the poor;
On pleasures' wings they ride.
With dishes fine their tables shine,
They live in princely style.
Those are the knaves who made us slaves
And sold Prince Edward Isle.

Each settler must pay rent.
So now you see the turning tide
That drove us to exile
Begin again to cross the main
And leave Prince Edward Isle.
The place was new, the roads were few
The people lived content;
The landlords came, their fields to claim,

But changes great have come of late
And brought some curious things;
Dominion men have brought us in,
With our own railway rings.
There's maps and charts and towns apart
And tramps of every style;
There's doctors mute and lawyers cute
Upon Prince Edward Isle.

So here's success to all who press
The question of Free Trade.
Join hand in hand, our cause is grand,
They're plainly in the shade.
The mainland route, the world throughout,
Take courage now, stand true,
My verse is run, my song is done,
Prince Edward Island, adieu.

Elaine Harrison has been involved in Island culture and life for more than thirty years. She has taught English in Island schools, published several books, and painted and written about the Island. Harrison's *I am an Island that Dreams* has been set to music by Jitky Snizkove, a Czech composer, and performed in Prague. This poem was also the basis of a CBC production, *This Land*. Deirdre Kessler captured an international audience with her popular Brupp series of young-adult novels about a cat who travels across Canada. Other notable Island wordsmiths include Elaine Hammond, Michael Hennessey, Copthorne Macdonald, Hugh MacDonald, J.J. Steinfeld and David Weale.

At the turn of the twentieth century, Prince Edward Island writer Lucy Maud Montgomery scribbled the following idea for a story in her notebook: "Elderly couple apply to orphan asylum for a boy. By mistake a girl is sent to them." The success of *Anne of Green Gables*, which was originally published in 1908, came as a complete surprise to Montgomery. She was astounded that the critics took "the book so seriously — as if it were meant for grown-up readers and not merely for girls."

More than eighty years later, Anne Shirley is the best-known fictional character in Canadian literature, and *Anne of Green Gables* has been read by more people than any other Canadian book. The *Anne* musical, which began in Charlottetown in 1965, has toured Canada and Japan; Hollywood has produced three *Anne* movies (1919, 1934, 1940); and several television miniseries, including the recent *Emily of New Moon* series, have been viewed in more than eighty countries, in at least sixteen different languages.

Maud, as she liked to be called, was born in 1874 in the little village of Clifton (now New London), where her father worked in the village general store. When Maud was twenty-one months old, her mother died of tuberculosis, and her father moved west to Saskatchewan to start a new life. Maud was sent to Cavendish to be raised by her mother's parents. Montgomery spent most of the next thirty-seven years in Cavendish, which became the setting for *Anne of Green Gables*. Maud later wrote, "Were it not for those Cavendish years, I do not think *Anne of Green Gables* would ever have been written."

Lucy Maud Montgomery

To earn a living, Montgomery became a school teacher. When her grandfather died in 1898, Maud left teaching (a career she did not enjoy) and returned to Cavendish to take care of her grandmother and to devote time to writing. Her first novel, *Anne of Green Gables*, became an immediate international success. After her grandmother died in 1911, Montgomery married Reverend Ewan Macdonald and moved to Ontario. There, despite the demanding duties of being a minister's wife and the mother of two sons, Montgomery published another nineteen novels. When Montgomery died in 1942, she was buried in Cavendish.

Theatre

Theatre has always been a popular form of entertainment for Islanders. Early in this century, many touring companies brought their productions to eager Island audiences. In rural areas, plays and concerts were exciting community events.

In 1964, the Confederation Centre of the Arts opened in Charlottetown. One of its first productions was a musical version of Montgomery's *Anne of Green Gables*. Other summer theatres include the King's Playhouse in Georgetown (rebuilt in 1984 after fire destroyed the original Victorian-style structure) and the Victoria Playhouse. French-language theatre is presented each summer at the Acadian Village at Mont-Carmel. Lively productions are also staged at Charlottetown's MacKenzie Theatre and the French-language school and community centre, Le carrefour de l'isle St. Jean. The Community Schools movement promotes drama, and Theatre Prince Edward Island assists both school and community groups.

Art

Perhaps the best-known Island artist is Robert Harris. His most famous painting is the study of the Fathers of Confederation, which was used on Canadian postage stamps, on Canadian National Railway dining car menus, and has been reproduced for classrooms across the country.

Harris was seven years old when his family emigrated from Wales in 1849 to Prince Edward Island. He later studied art in England, Boston and Paris, where he became an expert portrait painter. In 1879, Harris decided to devote his life to art. As his fame spread throughout Canada, Harris was invited to Montreal and Ottawa to paint portraits of the country's leading politicians and business people, and of the wives and children of wealthy Canadians. When the Canadian government decided to have a painting made of the Fathers of Confederation to celebrate the twentieth anniversary of the Confederation Conference, it selected Harris as the artist.

Harris found the job more difficult than he had thought it would be. Several of the politicians had died, and the others were twenty years older than they had been in 1864. Harris had played in the orchestra for the Confederation Conference at Charlottetown, but that had been when he was fifteen years old. Determined to be as accurate as possible, Harris sent questionnaires to people who had known the deceased politicians. He asked about the delegates' height, hair colour, whiskers, eyes, clothes and even the size of their hands. Harris met with those Fathers of Confederation who were still living and collected photographs of those who had died. The painting, which took Harris a year to finish, was completed in 1884 and brought him instant fame. It was hung in the Parliament Buildings at Ottawa. When the buildings were destroyed by fire in 1916, the painting was burned. By this time, Harris was sixty-seven years old, and his health and eyesight were poor. When asked to paint a replacement, the best he could do was to let the government buy the charcoal sketch from which he had made the original painting.

Many artists of national and international reputation live and work on the Island, which is home to many galleries and private studios. Artists such as Hilda Woolnough, Brian Burke, Erica Rutherford and Henry Purdy and craftspeople like Peter Jansen and Hedwig Kolesar have helped create a vibrant arts-and-crafts community in Prince Edward Island. The island's peaceful life and beautiful scenery seems to inspire creativity.

Genealogy

Genealogy is the third most popular hobby in North America, behind coin and stamp collecting. In the summers, especially, the Prince Edward Island Public Archives and Records Office and the Prince Edward Island Museum and Heritage Foundation cater to thousands of people interested in tracing their family trees. Novice genealogists benefit from the experience of these two organizations in their research of Island connections.

Sports

In the late 1800s, organized sports on the Island owed much of their development to the YMCA, the Caledonia Club and the Abegweit Athletic Club. The "Abbies" fielded teams in hockey, rugby, baseball, tennis, and track and field. Between 1900 and 1912, thanks largely to Bill Halpenny (Canadian pole-vault champion), James "Toby" MacMillan (Maritime sprint champion) and Michael Thomas (Maritime long-distance champion), the Abegweit Club won the Maritime track and field championship nine times. Bill Halpenny and Philip Blake McDonald (track) represented Canada in the Olympics — Halpenny in 1904 and 1912, and McDonald in 1924. In 1998, David (Eli) MacEachern, as part of Canada's two-man bobsleigh team, became the first Prince Edward Islander to bring home an Olympic gold medal.

Islanders love athletic competitions. The University of Prince Edward Island hockey, soccer and basketball teams receive extensive media and fan support. Recently, those teams have ranked among the best in Canada. Island hockey teams perform well in interprovincial competition, and Islanders keep close watch on the exploits of their National Hockey League stars. In recent times, Canada's smallest province has provided the NHL with such talents as Rick Vaive, Gerard Gallant, Forbes Kennedy, Allan MacAdam, Bob Stewart, Bobby and Billy MacMillan, Don Simmons, Errol Thompson and John Chabot.

Youngsters do well nationally in such diverse sports as squash, racquetball, baseball, golf and swimming. In 1951, Evelyn Henry of Keppoch became the first person to swim the treacherous Northumberland Strait, and thirty-eight years later Barb McNeill conquered the English Channel. The current number-three player in the squash world, Jonathon Power, got his start in P.E.I., and Lori Kane of Charlottetown is now one of the top players on the Ladies Professional Golf Association.

Horse Racing

Harness racing has earned P.E.I. the title "The Kentucky of Canada." The Island has more horses and more people involved in the horse industry per capita than any other province. Harness racing's roots go deep into the agricultural heritage of the Island. By the 1880s, more than two dozen race tracks dotted the countryside. When Lucy Maud Montgomery's Anne Shirley went to the races in Charlottetown, she wrote, "I don't think that I ought to go very often to horse races, because they *are* awfully fascinating. Diana got so excited that she offered to bet me ten cents that the red horse would win. I didn't because I wanted to tell Mrs. Allan all about everything, and I felt sure it wouldn't do to tell her that. It's always wrong to do anything you can't tell the minister's wife."

The introduction of nighttime pari-mutuel racing at the Charlottetown Driving Park in 1946 brought an end to many of the smaller Island tracks. Night racing meant that horse owners no longer had to take time off from work, and the general public could attend more easily. The crowning event of each year is the Gold Cup and

Saucer Race, which is held during Old Home Week. Since 1961, the Gold Cup and Saucer Parade has added to the lustre of this season-ending event. Joe O'Brien of Alberton (1917-1984) was one of North America's best-known harness racers and drove more sub-two-minute miles than any other harness driver in history. More recently, the lure of video lottery terminals and gambling casinos has reduced attendance at the Charlottetown Driving Park and at other harness-racing venues throughout the region.

SIXTEEN

The Guardian, July 22, 1939

Working wives are a menace to the general welfare, to the public health and to the morals of the nation.

A married woman's place is in the home ...

A married woman takes on a new name and new legal rights when she marries. She does not keep her identity as does a man ...

In being the superwomen they pretend, working wives cannot do two jobs well. They neglect either home or job. They cannot be dignified by the names of workers. They are chiselers, deserters from their post of duty, the home ...

Civilization can only advance when married women are protected in their natural career of homemaking.

A married woman should be proud of giving herself to her home instead of priding herself on holding a job in a little office.

The Struggle for Equality

Inequalities

"Why can't women be ministers, Marilla? I asked Mrs. Lynde that and she was shocked and said it would be a scandalous thing ... She hoped that we never would. But I don't see why. I think women would make splendid ministers ... I'm sure Mrs. Lynde can pray every bit as well ... and I've no doubt she could preach, too, with a little practice."

This statement was made by Anne Shirley, the heroine of Lucy Maud Montgomery's book *Anne of Green Gables*. Many Island girls must have asked similar questions. In pioneer times, women and men worked side by side. It wasn't until 1836 that women couldn't vote. As the division of labour became more pronounced, men's and women's roles in society changed. During most of the nineteenth and early twentieth centuries, women were not allowed to serve on juries. Females were not encouraged to go to school beyond the primary level, much less attend university. They were not permitted to become doctors or lawyers, nor allowed to vote, run for government or sit on school boards. According to the Election Act of the Dominion of Canada, an eligible voter in Canada was defined in 1890 as "A male person, including an Indian, and excluding a person of Mongolian or Chinese race ... No woman, idiot, lunatic or criminal shall vote."

On the Island, as elsewhere, women were thought to be capable of performing only a few jobs and were considered too weak, too emotional and too unintelligent to be politicians, business people, ministers, school principals or professionals. This severely limited their choices: they could marry and become housewives, or they could teach school, be maids, nurses, secretaries, store clerks, nuns or factory workers. Occupations such as nursing, dressmaking and public-school teaching came to be thought of as "women's work."

Women were expected — and sometimes told — to quit their jobs when they married. A married woman had few rights. Her husband controlled the family's money, including any income earned by the wife. Fathers had sole legal control over the children. Changes in the divorce law on the Island in the 1860s established a double standard by which husbands could gain divorce on the sole grounds of adultery, whereas wives had to demonstrate that their husbands had been guilty of adultery coupled with either sodomy, bigamy, rape, bestiality or desertion for more than two years. Perhaps as a result of this law, P.E.I. was the only jurisdiction in North America in which not a single divorce was granted in the last three decades of the nineteenth century. As late as 1941, only forty-one divorced people lived on the Island; the percentage of separated couples, however, was one of the highest in Canada.

Because women were limited in their choices by the written and unwritten laws made by men, they developed strategies to broaden their scope. They formed and managed charity organizations, women's institutes, and hospital and church auxiliary groups. Women raised funds through sales of baked goods, quilts and other handmade items to pay for the maps, globes, chalk and water

Island Divorces and Births

Years	Average Divorces	Births Per 1,000 People
1941 - 45	2	23.7
1946 - 50	21	30.5
1951 - 55	10	27.2
1956 - 60	4	26.6
1960 - 65	8	25.7
1966 - 70	45	18.9
1971 - 75	70	17.3
1976 - 80	139	16.1
1981 - 85	208	15.6
1986 - 90	254	15.2
1991 - 95	246	13.6

[P.E.I. Statistical Review, 1996]

Regulations for Nurses in 1887

In addition to caring for your patients, each nurse will follow these regulations:

1. *Daily sweep and mop the floors of your ward.*

2. *Keep an even temperature by bringing in coal for the day's work.*

3. *Each day fill kerosene lamps, clean chimneys and trim wicks. Wash windows once a week.*

4. *Each nurse will report every day at 7 AM and leave at 8 PM, except on the Sabbath when you will be off from noon to 2 PM.*

5. *Graduate nurses in good standing with the Director of Nurses will be given an evening off each week for courting purposes, or two evenings a week if you go regularly to church.*

6. *Any nurse who smokes, drinks liquor, gets her hair done at a beauty shop or goes to dance halls will give the Director of Nurses good reason to suspect her worth, intentions and honesty.*

buckets that were desperately needed by local schools. They looked after many of the details that held families and communities together. Women were closely in touch with the cycle of life, from midwifery to the preparation of the dead for burial.

Many women became involved in missionary organizations, for which they organized fundraising drives and served as missionaries in foreign fields. In 1884, for example, the Women's Baptist Missionary Union of the Maritime Provinces had twelve branches in Prince Edward Island, and Bay View sisters Martha and Dr. Zella Clark performed heroic work as missionary doctors in China at the turn of the twentieth century.

Women were paid less money than men for doing the same type of work. This was just as true for the women who worked in lobster canneries as it was for teachers. The regulations that surrounded women in the workplace were strict. In some factories, female workers were not allowed to mix with male workers. Factory owners told female workers what to wear and how to cut their hair.

The Right to Vote

In 1916, an important event occurred in the history of Prince Edward Island. The Women's Liberal Club was formed under Margaret Rogers Stewart and Elsie Inman. Stewart and Inman and eighty-eight other women decided it was time Island women had the right to vote. The Women's Liberal Club wrote for advice to suffragists such as Nellie McClung and Emily Murphy, who were leading the fight for the vote and equal status of women in Manitoba and Alberta. They decided that the best way to accomplish their goal was to convert men to their views. In a quiet way, this group of determined women began to change old ideas about women's place in society. They spoke about women's rights and needs to various groups across the Island, to members of government and to all the women they met.

The first major breakthrough came during the First World War. Many women took over jobs left by the men who went overseas to fight. They became involved in the Red Cross and in making clothes for the soldiers. They worked on assembly lines in factories, and dressed in overalls and trousers. They did "men's work" and did it well. Partly as a result of this success, but more for political reasons, women who had husbands or relatives in the army were allowed to vote in the 1917 Canadian elections. The next year, women all across Canada over the age of twenty-one received the right to vote in federal elections.

Unlike the situation in other provinces, Island women had made few attempts at enfranchisement prior to the war. When John Dewar proposed such a measure in the legislature in 1918, the male politicians decided to wait until the women demanded the right to vote in provincial elections. The Charlottetown Examiner, however, declared, "Can women perform aright the multifarious duties of the home, follow the fashions closely, give time to social matters, take a lively interest in current news and gossip, etc., and also attend closely to matters and questions of political importance?"

The Women's Liberal Club knew they could, and began to actively lobby the members of the legislature and to recruit help from the Women's Institutes, which had been formed in 1913. In response to several petitions in 1922, Premier John Bell announced that Island women should have the franchise because they voted in federal elections; they had helped win the war; it would help to broaden women's "subjects of conversation and study"; and the public would benefit from their advice on matters of morals, health and the family. Despite one member's complaint that a woman's "place is in the home, in the kitchen looking after home affairs," Island women received the franchise in 1922.

Not everyone was happy with this decision, especially not some men. Senator Elsie Inman described the problems some women had at this time:

> Most of the women were afraid of their husbands. The majority of husbands refused to let them vote. Well, I remember taking a woman — she said she'd vote, but she was scared to vote because her husband threatened her if he saw her at a poll. She was anxious to vote and I said, "Would he know you if you were dressed up in other clothes?" Well, she didn't think he would, so I went home and she was about my size. We wore veils in those days, so I took my clothes and coat and put the veil on her and took her to vote … I went to the door to get another woman to vote and her husband met me and said, "Get out of this, trying to lead my wife astray, you should be ashamed of this. You're from a nice family, and have a good husband, you should be ashamed of yourself."

Women Today

Gradually, women have been gaining equality with men in other areas than the right to vote. In 1965 in Prince Edward Island, women gained the privilege to sit on juries. Nine years later, the minimum wage was equalized for males and females. In 1977, the federal government passed a law to make it an offence to discriminate against women.

More and more women are employed in non-traditional jobs. In 1983 Leone Bagnall became the minister of education, and Marion Reid was Speaker of the House in 1990. When the Liberal Party won the 1993 provincial election, Catherine Callbeck became the first elected female premier in Canadian history. Ironically, the voters had little choice in this matter, as the leaders of the two main political parties were women. From 1993 to 1996, women held the six most senior legislative offices in the Island government: Catherine Callbeck was Premier, Marion Reid was Lieutenant Governor, Nancy

Guptill was Speaker, Major Margaret MacKinnon was Aide-de-Camp to the Lieutenant Governor, Pat Mella was Leader of the Official Opposition and Libby Hubley was Assistant Speaker. There are increasing numbers of women practising medicine and law, and more women in business or doing carpentry, truck driving and other work that traditionally has been done by men.

Today, women still face discrimination. Top business and professional jobs continue to be more difficult for women to obtain. Females are still expected to take "women's jobs" and are sometimes paid less money than men for doing work of equal value. Although there have been many changes in the way women are treated in society, there are still many injustices. These include continuing discrimination by employers based on gender and marital status, sexual harassment in the workplace, rape, battering, insufficient daycare facilities and inadequate maternity leave. Pension plans often leave women whose husbands predecease them with meagre funds upon which to exist. Senior citizens, the majority of whom are elderly women, require greater support, as do the growing number of single-parent families headed by women.

Brian L. Simpson

Women of Power (*Clockwise from bottom right:* Catherine Callbeck, Marion Reid, Nancy Guptill, Margaret MacKinnon, Pat Mella and Libby Hubley)

SEVENTEEN

Debki Dancers

Michael Rashed

A Multicultural Island

Although the Island is the most culturally and racially homogeneous Canadian province, more than sixty different nationalities are represented on Prince Edward Island. The Mi'kmaq arrived thousands of years ago. They were followed by the Acadians in the early eighteenth century, and then by English, Scottish and Irish settlers in the late eighteen and nineteenth centuries. Most of the other ethnic groups in P.E.I. have immigrated to the Island since the Second World War. Significantly, it was not until 1975 that the first non-British mayor of Charlottetown, Frank Zakem, who was born in Lebanon, was elected.

A small German settlement apparently existed briefly on the Island in the Acadian period, but it was not until the Loyalists arrived following the American Revolution that P.E.I. had a permanent German population. Today, the German population is spread from Cape Kildare to Souris, and they are integrated into the society around them. To avoid discrimination, many early German settlers anglicized their names — Henckells became Jenkins, Eichorns became Acorns, and Junkers became Younkers.

Lebanese people began to come to the Island in the late 1800s. The Christian Lebanese were experiencing persecution under the Turks. Many Lebanese heard about North America and decided they could create a better life for themselves in the New World. Families and, in some cases, whole villages emigrated to America. The first Lebanese settlers arrived in Prince Edward Island in the 1880s. Many of the young Lebanese men established themselves as "pack pedlars." These merchants travelled from farm to farm on foot or by horse and wagon, selling everything from tea to trousers. They provided a needed service for many farming families, who seldom got to town. Although the farmers were at first wary of the

Prince Edward Island Population Ethnic Origins, 1991

English:	29,465
Scottish:	16,660
French:	11,680
Irish:	10,155
Dutch:	1,250
German:	645
Aboriginal:	405
Other European:	345
Asian:	195
Total Population:	128,100

[Canada Year Book, 1997]

strangers, they soon began to look forward to the pedlars' visits, and offered food and lodging to them when they came. Through hard work, many of the merchants earned enough money to open small stores, some of which still exist today.

Prince Edward Island has become home to an increasing number of people of different racial and ethnic origins. The P.E.I. Multicultural Council has a visible presence in the Island community, and more efforts have been made to raise awareness about racism. In fact, Prince Edward Island elected Canada's first premier of Lebanese origin, Joe Ghiz, in 1986.

Acadian Culture: The Struggle to Survive

Prior to 1860, Acadians lived in their own communities and generally avoided contact with English-speaking settlers. One reason for this was their desire to keep their Acadian culture and traditions. Since Acadian school children were instructed almost solely in French, most Acadians could not speak English. In the 1860s and 1870s, the provincial government ordered Acadian schools to teach every subject (except French) in the English language. Acadian teachers and Roman Catholic priests fought against this attempt to destroy Acadian culture.

In the fall of 1859, a French-speaking priest from Lower Canada arrived on the Island to become pastor of Rustico, at the request of the bishop, who was short of priests to serve Acadian parishes. Father Georges-Antoine Belcourt, then fifty-six years old, had worked for twenty-eight years as a missionary among the Indians and Métis in Manitoba and Minnesota. Upon arriving in Rustico, Father Belcourt immediately set about improving the Acadians' quality of life. Island Acadians were generally very poor, had small farms and were in debt to the landlords. Father Belcourt first established the Catholic Institute of Rustico, a temperance society for men, which met regularly to hear lectures on economics, farming, science and geography. Father Belcourt used the Institute to start many other worthwhile projects.

One of the projects introduced by Belcourt was the creation of the Farmers' Bank of Rustico, the forerunner of the credit union movement in North America and the smallest chartered bank in Canada. The basis of the Rustico Bank was cooperation. Belcourt thought that by running their own bank, Acadian farmers would learn about economics and be able to borrow money more cheaply than they could elsewhere. It would also allow them to get loans for seed grain and additional farmland, and help maintain a spirit of independence in Acadian communities.

Another of Belcourt's ideas was to find farmland for the younger generation. He supervised an emigration project that sent a few hundred Acadians from the Island to settle in Lower Canada and New Brunswick. Today, many descendants of Island Acadians still live in Quebec and New Brunswick.

Father Belcourt also wanted to train bilingual teachers and thus help preserve the French language and Acadian culture. To achieve this, he established a French high school, complete with a library with a good selection of French books, which he operated for a few years until a sufficient number of suitable teachers were available.

The Acadian flag

Richard Furlong

In the middle of the nineteenth century, the rise of a sense of Acadian nationalism throughout the Maritimes helped Island Acadians in their struggle to preserve their own culture. In 1864, an Acadian college was built in New Brunswick, and a French newspaper, *Le Moniteur Acadien*, began in 1867. In the next several years, other French-language newspapers were started, including *L'Impartial* (1893-1915) in Tignish. The Acadian Teachers' Association, a home and school association, and the Saint Thomas Aquinas Society were created to promote French-language education. Maritime Acadians also met in large conventions to discuss various issues and to find ways to preserve their culture. An Acadian flag, anthem, patron saint and official feast day resulted from these conventions.

Without government assistance, French-speaking teachers or money, the Acadian leaders fought an uphill battle. Many Acadian children were forced to attend English-speaking classes. By 1966, only one-half of all Acadian people could read or understand French. In the 1960s, however, the Island government changed its educational policies. It decided that in districts with a large number of Acadians, classes could be taught in French. The first such area was Evangeline. Today, Acadian art and culture are experiencing a rebirth on the Island.

The Oldest Islanders

The Mi'kmaq have had even more problems than the Acadians in maintaining their culture. After the conquest, the British government was not as friendly towards the Mi'kmaq as the French authorities had been. Following the peace treaty of 1763, the British government gave small amounts of land to the Mi'kmaq in New Brunswick and Nova Scotia; however, on Prince Edward Island all the land — which once had belonged to the Mi'kmaq — was given away by lottery to wealthy British landlords.

To most British settlers and administrators, the Mi'kmaq were an invisible people. After two years of gathering information about the Island, Governor Walter Patterson reported in 1772 that there were "no Natives, or Indians, who either inhabit, or claim any right to" P.E.I. Since the number of Mi'kmaq was so small and no treaty had been negotiated with them, the government could safely ignore their presence. The British settlers themselves were quite willing to see the Mi'kmaq pass out of existence "like leaves before the autumn's blast."

For a while, the Mi'kmaq continued to roam the Island in search of game, but as European settlers increased in number, they cleared the forests, erected fences and killed the wild animals that the Mi'kmaq relied on to survive. When the Mi'kmaq were no longer able to move their camps freely from place to place, they asked the government for land of their own, but the government was unwilling to help. Finally, Sir James Montgomery, a wealthy British landlord, offered to let them live on Lennox Island rent-free in 1804.

The government thought that Lennox Island was a perfect spot. It would separate the Mi'kmaq from the settlers and prevent trouble. A Catholic missionary, Abbé de Callone, persuaded several Mi'kmaq families to settle year-round on Lennox Island, where they built a chapel, cleared several hectares of land and planted potatoes. Unfortunately, the land was not very fertile, as one-third of Lennox Island was swampy. Moreover, settlers came to Lennox Island to cut the wild hay in the marshes to feed their livestock. Despite Mi'kmaq complaints, in the 1820s, the marshland was rented to the settlers rather than to the Mi'kmaq, who could not pay for it. The Mi'kmaq asked the government to buy Lennox Island for them, but nothing was done. In addition to the work of Abbé de Callone, Baptist missionary Silas Rand lobbied the government to meet the spiritual and physical needs of the Mi'kmaq.

By the 1830s, no one was sure how many Mi'kmaq were living on the Island. Guesses ranged from two hundred to five hundred. It was difficult to determine the exact number because very few remained in one location for long. Hunting and fishing required them to move from place to place. Only a handful of families lived year-round on Lennox Island, although large numbers gathered there in July to celebrate Saint Anne's Day. Favourite camping grounds included Crapaud, Egmont Bay, Indian River, Morell, St. Peter's and near the Charlottetown harbour.

The Mi'kmaq hunted and fished for what food they could, and earned a meagre income selling firewood and goods crafted from wood, bark and cloth. The men fashioned barrels, furniture, ship

A Mi'kmaq Petition

The Mi'kmaq asked the government for land, food or money in return for the land that had been taken from them. An edited copy of the petition they sent to the government of Prince Edward Island in 1832 follows:

To the Great Leaders of Prince Edward Island

Fathers, — Before the white men crossed the great waters — our woods offered us food and clothes in plenty — the waters gave us fish — and the woods game — our fathers were hardy, brave and free — we knew no want — we were the only owners of the land.

Fathers, — When the French came to us they asked us for land to set up their wigwams — we gave it freely — In return they taught us new arts — protected and cherished us — sent holy men who taught us Christianity — who made books for us — and taught us to read them — that was good — and we were grateful.

Fathers, — When your fathers came and drove away our French fathers — we were left alone, — our people were sorry, but they were brave — they raised the war cry — and took up the tomahawk against your fathers. — Then your fathers spoke to us — and said, put up the axe — we will protect you — we will become your fathers. — Our fathers and your fathers had long talks around the council fire — the hatchets were buried — and we became friends.

Fathers, — They promised to leave us some of our land — but they did not — They drove us from place to place like wild beasts — that was not just.

Fathers, — Our tribe in Nova Scotia, Canada, New Brunswick and Cape Breton, have land on which their families are happy. — We ask of you, Fathers, to give us a part of the land that was once our fathers' — where we may raise our wigwams without disturbance — and plough and sow — that we may live, and our children also — else, Fathers, you may soon see not one drop of Indian blood in this Island. Where is our land? — we have none. —

Fathers, we are poor — do not forget us — remember the promises your fathers made to ours. Fathers, we salute you.

(Signed) Louis Francouis Alguimou,
Piel Jaques,
Oliver Thoma,
Peter Tony,
Micael Michell.

fittings, brooms, axe handles, toy bows and arrows, snowshoes and canoes. The women made beautiful beaded cloth goods, boxes with porcupine quillwork mosaics and birchbark utensils embroidered with animal hair. Woodsplint baskets, made by the whole family, were the most popular items. When all else failed, the Mi'kmaq were forced to beg for food and clothing.

In the mid-1850s, the government appointed two Indian commissioners, Theophilus Stewart and Henry Palmer, to encourage the Mi'kmaq to engage in farming and thus become self-sufficient. The commissioners were given a small budget to care for the Mi'kmaq's needs. In 1865, Stewart attended the annual meeting of the Aborigines Protection Society in London, England. Although this society was dedicated to helping Aboriginal groups around the world, it had generally ignored the Maritimes. Stewart's visit changed its priorities. Five years later, the Aborigines Protection Society purchased Lennox Island for the Mi'kmaq and helped them survey the land and build roads.

When P.E.I. entered Confederation in 1873, the Mi'kmaq came under the control of the federal government. The Canadian government was not very concerned about the Mi'kmaq. By 1880, their numbers had fallen to 266, and it appeared that they might disappear from the Island. But the Mi'kmaq did not die out. They survived by hunting geese in the spring; fishing and digging shellfish in the summer; and making axe handles, baskets and oars in the winter to sell to nearby farms. By 1917 there were reserves at Lennox Island, Morell, Scotchfort and Rocky Point.

A large number of Mi'kmaq volunteered for service during the two world wars and worked in war-related industries, even though they had to give up their Indian status, and the government support this status entitled them to, in order to serve in the Canadian military. Gradually, more and more Mi'kmaq discarded their traditional clothing and way of life, and adopted the values and lifestyles of the surrounding society.

In the late 1940s, the federal government coerced the Mi'kmaq into living on Lennox Island by providing social assistance only to those who resided on this reserve. Lennox Island had its own elementary school, but older students had to attend a residential high school in Schubenacadie, Nova Scotia. Here, children were

The Guardian

Mi'kmaq children celebrate St. Anne's Day

separated from their parents for the school year, all instruction was in English, and children were severely punished for speaking their own language or practising their cultural and spiritual traditions.

The Mi'kmaq were denied the right to vote (unless they were war veterans who had lost their status and therefore were not considered "Indian" by the government), were prohibited from drinking alcohol and were not legally considered citizens until 1957. Until 1985, Aboriginal women who married non-Natives lost their Indian status (as did their offspring), whereas non-Native women who married status Indians gained Indian status (as did their children).

In 1973, the government built a causeway between Lennox Island and P.E.I. No longer isolated, and finally given more freedom to administer its affairs, the Lennox Island Band began to provide for itself. It started an oyster co-op, followed by peat moss, handicrafts and blueberry industries. In 1972, the Morell, Scotchfort and Rocky Point Reserves formed the Abegweit Band, and embarked on their own economic projects. The Mi'kmaq language is now taught in the Lennox Island school, and the Mi'kmaq are actively attempting to preserve their traditions.

When asked what the Mi'kmaq want, John Joe Sark of Lennox Island replied that they were "looking for basically the same things all of us are looking for. First of all, to be put on an equal footing with you. We do a little of everything now, but we do not have sufficient land base or resources ... We have to have our own type of government. We are sophisticated enough to find solutions to our own problems. Our future lies with developing along with our neighbours around us, being allowed to change that lifestyle at our own speed."

EIGHTEEN

The dunes at Cavendish

Lionel Stevenson

The Island Way

For the last several decades, Prince Edward Island has been trying to decide where its destiny lies. Some Islanders point to the Island's high unemployment rate and an average income that falls well below the national level to support their demands that P.E.I. adopt all the latest technological and economic advances. Other people wish to return to past values, and worry that the Island is losing its separate identity and endangering its environment by adopting non-Island ways. These conflicting views are particularly apparent in regard to tourism, land use and the fixed link.

Tourism

Since the 1880s, there has been a concerted effort to develop the Island as a tourist mecca based upon its natural beaches, lush rolling countryside, cultural heritage and its people's congeniality. In 1885, for example, a travel writer noted, "It is the influx of such visitors, with pockets popularly supposed to be lined with gold, that the Island may reasonably look for a return of some of its vanished prosperity." Gradually, the number of tourists has increased from 11,000 in 1924 to 278,000 in 1963, and to over 1,000,000 in 1997.

Perhaps the most unexpected tourists to the Island are the Japanese who flock to Cavendish to visit a recreated home of a Canadian girl who never existed, and to examine objects she might have used had she been a real girl. Many Japanese women between the ages of seventeen and twenty-four break into tears when they first enter Anne's "home." Some Japanese tourists offer money to Island girls for a lock of their red hair. When a Japanese travel magazine asked its readers what location they would most like to visit, Prince Edward Island ranked fourth behind New York, Paris and London. In 1996, over 25,000 Japanese tourists visited the Island.

The Japanese attraction to *Anne of Green Gables* may be attributed to the universal appeal of Montgomery's novels, the situation in Japan at the end of the Second World War when *Anne of Green Gables* was first translated into Japanese and the cultural "fit" between Japanese beliefs and the values expressed in Montgomery's novels.

Lucy Maud Montgomery was among the first wave of writers to approach her work from a child's perspective. "It was a labour of love," Montgomery noted in her diary after completing *Anne of Green Gables*. The characters, such as Marilla, with her stern conscience and warm heart, or Matthew, who has trouble expressing his feelings, are recognizable in all places and times. Anne herself had human flaws, and readers can identify with her feelings of rejection and longing for approval. Montgomery revealed the shortcomings of the adult world, the restrictions of convention and the importance children attach to such seeming trifles as puffed sleeves, eating ice cream or sleeping in a bed in the spare room. "When I am grown up," Anne informed her best friend Diana Barry, "I'm always going to talk to little girls as if they were, too, and I'll never laugh when they use big words. I know from sorrowful experience how that hurts one's feelings."

Japan lay in ruins after the Second World War. Millions of people had been killed, the victorious Americans occupied the country and age-old traditions were endangered. Japanese children needed cheerfulness, optimism and hope, all of which could be found in abundance in *Anne of Green Gables*. Teachers and parents welcomed Anne as a person who provided readers with a positive role model of how to live in less than ideal circumstances. Like many Japanese girls at that time, Anne Shirley was an orphan. Despite her inauspicious start in life, Anne was always optimistic and cheerful, and through honesty, perseverance and the goodness of her heart, her well-meaning actions brought happiness to those around her. On her way to Mrs. Spencer's, in what Anne dreaded might be her last day at Green Gables, Anne informed Marilla, "I've made up my mind to enjoy this drive. It's been my experience that you can nearly always enjoy things if you make up your mind firmly that you will."

Anne of Green Gables is popular in Japan also because of the many similarities between Japanese culture and the values and traditions of Montgomery's Avonlea. The Island's natural beauty fascinates Japanese people, and Montgomery's vivid descriptions and idealization of nature closely parallel the Japanese love of nature. In both Japan and Avonlea, people possess a sense of community in which everyone knows where they fit and what is expected of them, and where hard work and frugality are pre-eminent virtues. In small islands such as Japan and P.E.I. it is necessary to live peacefully with your neighbours, including sacrificing personal desires for the welfare of the community. As the Japanese proverb, "The Nail That Sticks Up Shall Be Hammered Down" indicates, the basic characteristic of the Japanese is submission of the individual to the society. This is also a common theme in Montgomery's novels. For instance, Anne postpones her desire to attend college in order to look after Marilla.

Anne of Green Gables continues to be popular among Japanese women because in many ways the Japan of today is similar to Prince Edward Island in 1900. The novel may be interpreted as a criticism of Island society. Rather than praising Island life, Montgomery expresses her secret critical thoughts about the conventions, religious practices and the oppressive nature of Prince Edward Island society. The lack of privacy is evident in the opening chapter. Matthew

Gord Johnston Photography

Anne of Green Gables is staged at the Confederation Centre of the Arts in Charlottetown each summer

Cuthbert cannot even drive in his carriage without escaping the notice and speculations of Rachel Lynde, who was "forever sitting at her window, keeping a sharp eye on everything that passed." The Anne novels are a subtle condemnation of the restrictive nature of Avonlea society, where convention and custom ruled everyone's conduct. Marilla, who was so repressed that she was scarcely able to laugh, believed it was extremely important that Anne conform to society, and "conceived it her duty to drill Anne into a tranquil uniformity."

Montgomery's criticisms of conformity find a resonance in women living in Japanese society today. Similar to Anne Shirley, Japanese women live in an extremely conservative society in which all actions are strictly bound by convention. Like Anne, who imagined she wore a long nightgown with frills around the neck, instead of the "fearfully skimpy" nightdress she did wear, Japanese girls seek escape through their imaginations — by daydreaming or fantasizing. Japanese girls can identify with Anne's many mistakes and with her desire to pursue her own life. Marilla's strictness and devotion to duty is also easily recognizable amongst adult Japanese. As a result, every year several dozen Japanese couples get married in Prince Edward Island and tens of thousands of Japanese visit the Island in the summer.

Despite the fact that tourism provides many jobs and has become the province's most important industry, not everyone has been happy with its growth. Ever since the 1908 debate about allowing automobiles on the roads, Islanders have agonized over how much to cater to visitors at the expense of traditional customs. The tourist literature emphasizes P.E.I.'s pastoral nature and stresses that it offers an escape from the cares of city life. Yet, as more and more tourists travel to the Island, traffic jams, parking problems, air pollution and petty crime tend to destroy this idyllic environment. As the number of tourists increases, the unspoiled landscape is damaged: precious sand dunes are destroyed, cottages border the shoreline where farms once stood, commercial strips detract from the picturesque scenery and roadside signs advertise water slides and miniature castles. The conflict between modernization and traditional values typifies the pull between old and new. In 1974, Kings County successfully opposed the creation of a national park in the eastern end of the county. The Land Use Commission has several times refused to allow commercial development on prime agricultural land. At other times, however, the jobs created by golf courses, theme parks and water slides have carried the day.

Land Use

Much of the debate about the Island's future centres on some residents' conviction that the Island's economy and values rest with the rural independent farmer. In reality, however, the size of Island farms has steadily increased throughout this century, while the number of farmers has declined. Crop specialization and the rise of such large marketing and processing firms as Cavendish Farms have eroded the farmers' independence.

Concerned with the decline of the rural family farm and the threat posed to the environment by large-scale farming, several Island historians and their supporters sought to return Prince Edward Island to its "golden age" in the 1860s, when the people supposedly valued conservation, self-reliance and community. In 1979, this group successfully fought for a temporary ban on the construction of new shopping malls, which they felt were threatening to undermine the traditional country store. They were less successful, however, in their attempt to prevent school consolidation, which they believed would seriously weaken smaller rural communities. This time, it was the allure of modernization that prevailed.

The question of land use also reveals the pull between the desire for a better material life and the desire for the quiet rustic life of the countryside. In the early 1970s, fears that prime agricultural land was falling under the control of people "from away" awakened old memories of absentee landlords. In 1972, despite arguments that individuals should be free to dispose of their land to the highest bidder, government legislation required non-residents to gain cabinet approval for sales of land exceeding 4 hectares (10 acres) or 99 metres (330 feet) of shorefront property. Since then, the provincial government has passed several laws designed to preserve agricultural land for agricultural use, and it has singled out certain areas for special protection.

In the 1980s, concerned groups lobbied for effective legislation to prevent agricultural land from being acquired by large corporations. "The greatest threat to the family farm and to rural communities," declared the National Farmers Union, "is the encroachment into the field of farm production by industrial corporations." The government responded in 1982 by limiting corporate landholdings to 1,200 hectares (3,000 acres); however, it set no limit on how many hectares (acres) a firm could lease. Today, corporations such as McCain Foods and Cavendish Farms dominate the agricultural scene, and many people fear that the push toward potato monoculture will adversely change the landscape and destroy the natural environment of Prince Edward Island.

Early in 1990, the provincial government signed agreements with McCain Foods and Irving-owned Cavendish Farms that allowed the companies to build two potato processing plants that would employ several hundred workers. Once again, conservative and liberal beliefs clashed over the benefits of these changes. The processing plants' supporters revelled in the attention of such large companies. At the reception held for the McCain Foods' announcement, the guests dined on smoked salmon and shrimp impaled on watermelon. *The Guardian* editorialized:

> *This is news almost too good to comprehend ... After decades of shipping mainly raw produce and watching other provinces and countries process and profit from the added value, Prince Edward Island can smile — finally — at future prospects for the industry.*

Urban Laughlin, district director of the National Farmers Union, however, spoke of the threat the large processing plants posed to Island farmers and questioned the government's commitment to the family farm. He called for anti-vertical integration laws and demanded that the government concern itself with the disintegration of Island topsoil.

Public concern about land use and land deterioration is ever increasing. Many factors contribute to the public's growing concern: rapid expansion of the potato industry; pesticide use; industrial-scale farming and forestry; and pressures on the land from tourism, aquaculture, new agricultural products and settlement patterns. In response to these concerns, the government established a Round Table on Resource Land Use and Stewardship. In its report, released in 1997, The Round Table called for a renewed dialogue on the Island's environment and issued 87 recommendations designed to promote improved resource land use. "Perhaps our society has lost sight of what is important in this time of uncertainty, when so much energy is focused on the here and now," the sixteen members of the committee concluded. "Everyone is looking for a quick fix; unfortunately, there is none ... We live in a healthy environment, but unless we gain greater control over the economic forces that are shaping our Island, we risk destroying the very foundation of our economy."

The report paid particular attention to potato farming and its heavy use of chemicals, hedgerow removal and poor crop rotation, mechanical tree-harvesting, pesticide use, strip developers, water contamination and the need to protect wildlife habitat. The Atlantic Salmon Federation supported the Round Table's conclusion, particularly the suggestions that a buffer zone be established along Island waterways and that livestock be excluded from all rivers and streams. "A buffer zone is not only beneficial to the many wildlife species that live along waterways," the Federation noted, "it can also filter out some of the topsoil that makes its way from agricultural fields and unpaved highways each year. Although some streams regularly turn a brilliant red after each rainfall, this is not a natural occurrence. Silt and sand are choking our rivers, filling our ponds and destroying habitat for fish and wildlife which depend on these habitats."

Time will tell if this report will be more successful than its 1973 and 1990 predecessors.

The Fixed Link

In the late 1980s, the issue of a fixed link between Prince Edward Island and the mainland became a priority for the federal and provincial governments. The provincial government's 1989 fixed-link plebiscite forced Islanders to rethink their future. Since a fixed link would affect agriculture (cheaper transportation), fishing (possible environmental damage), tourism (easier access) and the number of visitors to the Island (quality of life), the issue aroused intense controversy. Although much of the debate focused on economic matters, a major difference was each side's view of "progress." The slogans of the two opposing groups illustrated their priorities. The pro-link platform's was "Islanders for a Better Tomorrow," whereas the anti-link people called themselves "Friends of the Island." Proponents of a stronger economy and a better materialistic lifestyle conflicted with defenders of the environment and the "Island way of life."

The Northumberland Strait has been more of a psychological than a physical buffer. According to Professor David Weale of the University of Prince Edward Island, giving up this insularity would mean trading the province's identity for an uncertain future. "The problem of low incomes and high unemployment which we share with the entire Atlantic region had nothing to do with our insularity," he wrote in 1988. "We offer some contrast to the boring, commercial, mass culture of North America. We also have a place to live that is wonderfully free from congestion and pollution."

Although almost 60 percent of Islanders voted in favour of some type of a fixed link, environmental and other concerns threatened to postpone construction indefinitely as both sides debated the wisdom of a fixed link, as well as the advantages and disadvantages of tunnels versus bridges. As writer and activist Lorraine Begley wrote in 1993, "There have been times over the past years when Islanders, in their individual disgust with the deafening drone of commentary on the fixed-link issue, have switched off their radios and televisions, refused to buy newspapers if the words 'fixed link' appeared anywhere on the front page and covered their ears to coffee-shop conversation if those dreaded words came up."

The worries were legion. Some people predicted that the massive piers required to support a bridge would prevent the ice from leaving Northumberland Strait for up to two weeks longer than usual, thus lowering the water and air temperatures in the spring and harming the oyster, clam, lobster and herring industries. Others were concerned that bridge construction would endanger wildlife and plant species, pollute groundwater resources, increase the danger of chemical spills, disturb the nesting and feeding sites of migratory birds, and that night lights on the bridge would mesmerize small birds in flight and cause them to crash. Marshes would be polluted. Concrete and steel production would threaten the environment.

Many Islanders worried about the impact the projected increase in tourists would have on Island communities or that easy access to the mainland would destroy Island commerce. Author Sharon Fraser wrote, "When you live in Prince Edward Island, your life rhythms are attuned to the ferry schedules. Arrival and departure times of the ferries — including hours of waiting time — become part of your consciousness, announced, as they are, on radio stations as regularly as weather forecasts and time checks are in other places. And when your ferry docks at Borden, you're home — even though you might have another hour-and-a-half drive to get to where you live."

The plebiscite in 1989 was the fourth time in Island history that the idea of a fixed link had been discussed seriously, and this time the proponents of the link did not intend to lose. A bridge would replace the traffic bottlenecks at both ends of the ferry route, allow Islanders to commute regularly to the mainland, increase the number of tourists and lower transportation costs. Although final approval hinged on the results of environmental studies, construction began in 1995.

Strait Crossing, the international consortium chosen to construct one of the most innovative engineering projects ever undertaken in Canada, paid particular attention to the environment. For example, it created six osprey nesting platforms on high poles that soon doubled the number of nesting pairs of osprey in the area; it also developed a 2.2-hectare (5.4-acre) waterfowl habitat. To keep dredging at the bottom of Northumberland Strait to a minimum, the company used radio signals from several global positioning satellites to place the pier shafts for the bridge with an accuracy of 2 centimetres (1 inch). Strait Crossing employed both sonar imaging and divers to monitor this work, and scows transported the dredged material to a site off Amherst Cove.

The bridge was fabricated in huge staging yards in New Brunswick and Prince Edward Island. In New Brunswick, Strait Crossing erected a 500-metre-long (545 yards) jetty to allow the *Svanen*, a huge twin-hulled floating crane that had to lift components up to 90 tonnes in weight, to remain in deep water and still pick up materials for the bridge. All the components for the bridge were made of steel-reinforced, high-strength concrete, further strengthened and linked together with high-tensile-strength steel tendons. In 1996, a helicopter was brought on site to pour concrete, help in construction and shuttle some of the 600 workers back and forth every day.

The finished bridge employed over 2,400 workers at its peak, used 478,000 cubic metres (626,180 cubic yards) of concrete, and dredged 277,000 cubic metres (362,870 cubic yards) of materials from the strait. The maximum elevation above sea level of this cantilevered bridge is 60 metres (195 feet). It measures 11 metres (36 feet) from guardrail to guardrail, has two 3.75-metre (12-foot)

The Confederation Bridge under construction

John Sylvester

traffic lanes, two 1.75-metre (5.5-foot) shoulders, and 1.1 metre-high (3.5 feet) barrier walls. To keep drivers alert, three curves help eliminate the hypnotic effect of straight lines. Other safeguards include 17 emergency call boxes and video surveillance cameras, changeable speed limit and message signs, equipment to monitor wind velocity and in-pavement sensors to detect ice formation. Shuttle buses transport pedestrians and cyclists across the bridge. At a normal driving speed of 80 kilometres (50 miles) per hour, it takes twelve minutes to cross the bridge.

Confederation Bridge was completed in June 1997. This 12.9-kilometre (8-mile) bridge is one of the longest continuous multis-pan bridges and the longest bridge over ice-covered water in the world. The project put more than $1 billion into the economy of Atlantic Canada, and additional money was set aside to compensate the 540 permanent ferry workers who lost their jobs and the fishers who would be affected by the bridge, and to provide alternate economic opportunities for Borden and Cape Tormentine, the towns at either end of the old ferry route.

It is too soon to determine the long-term impact of the bridge on the Island's economy, land use and way of life. The number of tourists increased in 1997 to over one million, but many of them came to see the Confederation Bridge. In 1990, fisher Steve Jones told the Environmental Assessment Panel, "After the thrill of expansion is gone and after the rumble of the big trucks is silent; after the newly built roads have grown up in alders again; after the line-ups at the take-outs are gone; after the fat paychecks are gone and when the bars are no longer crowded and you know almost everyone in them; when the cars going by contain men wearing baseball caps instead of hard hats and suits; when the work camps are quiet and decrepit and run down; when the entrepreneurs are back to square one; when Cape Tormentine is a ghost town and Cape Jourimain [the staging area in New Brunswick] is a string of last chance gas stations; what then?" Time will tell!

Small Is Beautiful

Despite attempts to resist change, P.E.I. has not been immune to the influences of the outside world. In fact, many of the people who trumpet the benefits of traditionalism come "from away." Having experienced life elsewhere, they chose to remain on the Island and now struggle vigorously to protect its way of life. However, it should be remembered that only 10 percent of the population is actively engaged in agriculture, and that tourism ranks either first or second in generating provincial income.

Public-service jobs provide incomes for a larger proportion of the population than in any other province, and the provincial government relies on its federal counterpart for much of its revenues. Although the Island might seem overgoverned for a province of only 130,000 people, it possesses a sort of direct democracy. Each elected member to the provincial government, for example, represents about 4,000 citizens. In Ontario, by contrast, each provincial member serves over 70,000 people. The people in Prince Edward Island know and have access to their elected representatives. The resulting feeling that they can affect government policies explains why Prince Edward Island usually has the highest voting turnout ratio in Canada. Perhaps the Island way of life is worth the struggle.

Index

O

Ontario, 95, 98, 122
Orwell, 37, 56, 58
Ottawa, 100, 104, 151
Oughton, The, 58
Oulton, Robert, 105-106
Owen, L.C., 90

P

Palmer, E., 81, 97-98
Patriot, The, 101
Patterson, Walter, 61-62, 65, 166
Peake, James, 90
Pearce, Patrick, 76-78
Pinette, 37
Pioneer, The, 91
Plebiscite, fixed link, 7, 179, 181
Point Prim, 58
Polly, The, 58
Pope, J.C., 87, 90
Pope, W.H., 96-98
Population, 10, 12, 43, 46, 61-63, 67, 93, 99, 104-105, 163-164, 183
Port Hill, 90, 92
Port LaJoye, 32, 34-36, 41, 44-46
Posse, 83-84
Potatoes, 13, 14, 69, 86, 122, 178
Potato Growers Association, 124
Poutrincourt, Jean de, 30
Pownal, 88
Prince County, 49-50, 92, 106, 125-126
Prince Edward Island, The, 116
Prince Edward Island Cooperative Egg and Poultry Association, 124
Princetown, 49-50
Processing, 89, 125, 177-178
Protestant, 51, 55, 57, 63-64, 142
    See also Religion

Province House, 74, 94, 97
Provincial government, 84, 101, 110, 122-123, 143, 164, 177-178, 182-183

Q

Quebec, 49, 95, 98, 137, 165
    See also Confederation
Queen Victoria, The, 96
Queens County, 49-50, 130
Quit rent, 50-51, 63-64, 79

R

Railway, 100-101, 104, 148, 150
Rayner, B.I., 106
Rayner, Silas, 106
Red Cross, 108, 136-138, 159
Relief, The, 130
Religion, 20, 38, 57, 68, 71, 73
    missionaries, 19-20, 42, 158
    priests, 20, 34, 38-39, 41-43, 164-165
    See also Protestant, Roman Catholic
Rent, 76, 79-80, 83, 148
Responsible government, 81-82, 99
Richards, William, 90
Rocky Point, 48, 169, 170
Rogers, David, 87
Rogers, Keith S., 119
Rollo Bay, 67
Rollo, Lord, 43-44, 46, 48
Roma, Jean Pierre, 32-36
Roman Catholic, 20, 29, 31, 34, 39, 41, 43, 51, 55-57, 64, 68, 71, 73, 124, 142-143, 164, 167
    See also Religion, Saint Anne's Day
Round Market, The, 74
Royalties, 50, 81

S

Saint Anne's Day, 41, 167, 170
Saint Pierre, Comte de, 32
Saskatchewan, 100
Savage Harbour, 21, 32
School consolidation, 143, 177
Schurman, M.F., 87
Scotchfort, 51, 57, 169, 170
Scots
    Gaelic, 68, 72-73
    Highlanders, 58, 68, 73
    Scottish Catholics, 51, 55, 68
    Scottish Protestants, 51, 55, 64
Scurvy, 41
Selkirk, Earl of, 54, 57
Selkirk land purchase, 82
Senate, 98
Settlers, 33, 40, 43, 51-52, 54,
    56, 58, 62-63, 67, 69-70, 93,
    131, 146, 163, 167, 178
    English, 163-164, 166-167
    French, 30, 32, 35-36, 42-43
Shellfish, 13-14, 21, 24, 69, 89,
    169
Shipbuilding, 89-93, 99, 104
Shipyards, 90
Size, 11-12
Slaves, 62
Souris, 34-35, 90, 100
South Uist Island, 55
South West River, 87
Spartan, The, 102
St. Dunstan's College, 73, 143
St. Eleanors, 88, 127
St. John's Island, 46-59, 60-65
St. Peter's Bay, 87
St. Peter's Harbour, 32, 34
Stanhope, 51, 54, 55
Stanley, The, 114
Stevens, Philip, 50
Stewart, Peter, 64
Stewart, Robert, 51
Straight Crossing, 181

Sturgeon River, 34
Suffragists, 159
Summerside, 50, 88, 90, 123, 137
Svanen, The, 180

T

Tenant League, The, 83-84
Tenants, 58, 64, 77, 79-80, 82-
    83
Thirteen Colonies, 56
Tignish, 67, 100, 105, 124-125,
    127, 166
Tourism, 14-15, 173-176, 178-
    181
Townshend, Lord James, 79
Tracadie, 32-33, 51, 55-56
Treaty of Utrecht, 30
Trois Rivières, 32-36
Tryon, 37, 56
Tuplin, Robert, 106

U

Unemployment, 58, 113, 128,
    179
    See also Employment
United States, 36, 46, 56, 58,
    95, 99-100, 104, 110, 191
    See also American Revolu-
    tion, George Washington
University of Prince Edward Is-
    land, 73-74, 143, 153, 191

V

Vernon River, 56, 83
Violet, The, 45
Voting, 15, 62-63, 68, 110,
    170, 183
    high turnout, 15, 183
    See also Elections, Women's
    rights

W

Y

Professor Douglas Baldwin came "from away" to teach history at the University of Prince Edward Island in 1979. Since then, he has been researching the facts and folklore that shape the history of Canada's smallest province. Dr. Baldwin has written numerous books and articles on many facets of Island life, from banking history to urban development to public health and nursing history, and has lectured in Canada, Japan, Great Britain and the United States. Baldwin's Island publications include *She Answered Every Call: The Life of Public Health Nurse, Mona Gordon Wilson, 1894-1981* (Indigo Press, 1997); *The Land of Anne: A History of Prince Edward Island* (published in Japanese, translated by Kazuo Kimura, 1995); *Expected and Unexpected: Childbirth in Prince Edward Island, 1827-1857: The Case Book of Dr. John Mackieson* (St. John's: Occasional Papers in the History of Medicine, 1992); *Gaslights, Epidemics and Vagabond Cows: Charlottetown in the Victorian Era* (Ragweed Press, 1988), edited with Dr. Thomas Spira. Dr. Baldwin now teaches in the history department at Acadia University in Nova Scotia. He is working on his thirteenth book, a documentary history of sports in North America in the 1930s.

Best of Ragweed Press

From Red Clay & Salt Water: Prince Edward Island & Its People, John Sylvester. "Sylvester has lovingly captured the light and colour of the Island's gently varied landscape, and played them against portraits of Islanders ... Their words and Sylvester's pictures make Prince Edward Island a vivid reality for those of us who 'come from away.' " *Islands: An International Magazine*
ISBN 0-921556-40-3 $27.95

Making It Home: Memoirs of J. Angus MacLean, J. Angus MacLean. Decorated World War II veteran, politician, federal cabinet minister, provincial premier, sheep farmer and steward of the land, J. Angus MacLean was a true Canadian hero. "*Making It Home* is a wonderful reflection of a life spent serving the public." *Eastern Graphic*
ISBN 0-921556-73-X $19.95

An Island Alphabet, Erica Rutherford. Internationally renowned artist Erica Rutherford captures the beauty and unique charm of Island life in a gorgeous memento from the Maritimes. Full colour art and large format make it the perfect gift.
ISBN 0-921556-44-6 $14.95

Lobster in my Pocket, Deirdre Kessler, illustrated by Brenda Jones. This wonderful story of the magical friendship between a young girl and a talking lobster is a perennial favourite with visitors to Atlantic Canada.
ISBN 0-920304-73-7 $7.95

Ragweed Press titles are available at quality bookstores. Ask for our titles at your favourite local bookstore. Individual, prepaid orders may be sent to: Ragweed Press, P.O. Box 2023, Charlottetown, Prince Edward Island, Canada, C1A 7N7. Please add postage and handling ($4.00 for the first book and $1.00 for each additional book) to your order. Canadian residents add 7% GST to the total amount. GST registration number R104383120. Prices are subject to change without notice.